DECISIONS! DECISIONS! DECISIONS!

Steve Lawhead

This book is designed to provide you with practical and spiritual help for making good decisions. You can read it by yourself or study it with a group. A leader's guide, containing visual aids (SonPower Multiuse Transparency Masters), and Rip-Off sheets (student activity booklets) are available from your local Christian bookstore or from the publisher.

VICTOR BOOKS a division of SP Publications, Inc.
WHEATON, ILLINOIS 60187

Offices also in
Whitby, Ontario, Canada
Amersham-on-the-Hill, Bucks, England

All Bible quotations are from the *New International Version*, © 1978 by the New York International Bible Society. Used by permission. Other quotations are from the *New American Standard Bible* (NASB), © 1960, 1962, 1963, 1968, 1971, 1972, 1973, 1975, by The Lockman Foundation.

Library of Congress Catalog Number: 83-51365
ISBN: 0-88207-591-8

Recommended Dewey Decimal Classification: 248.83
Suggested Subject Heading: YOUTH—RELIGIOUS LIFE

© 1984, Steve Lawhead. All rights reserved.
Printed in the United States of America.

CONTENTS

1. Whose Life Is It Anyway? 7
2. What Does God Want? 18
3. Free To Choose, but Not Alone 27
4. When Decisions Go Bad 37
5. Asking The Right Questions 48
6. A Matter of Choice 60
7. Look Before You Leap 73
8. Waiting and Debating 86
9. The Mind of Christ 97
10. Time to Act 103
11. Improving Your Foresight 112
12. Follow-through 121

The author wishes to acknowledge the work of James D. Jorgensen and Timothy F. Fautsko. Their book, *Quid: How to Make the Best Decisions of Your Life* (Walker & Co., 1978), inspired some of the ideas in this book.

This book is dedicated to
my Mom,
who never steered me wrong.

1
WHAT DOES GOD WANT?

Uncle Elmo thinks you ought to be a fireman. Aunt Agatha insists that a voice like yours belongs in the grand opera. Your dad says that he always hoped you would carry on the family tradition and go to Slippery Rock College. Your mom says you're going to be a doctor. Little brother thinks you would make a great astronaut. Grandma thinks you ought to get married and start a family of your own so she can be a great-grandmother.

Everyone has designs for your life. From your sixth-period algebra teacher to your friendly neighborhood army recruiter, *everyone* seems to have just the right plan for you. If you know 100 people, chances are you will get 100 different opinions about what you ought to do with yourself at any given moment.

The only person who doesn't know for sure what you should do is you!

8 / Decisions! Decisions! Decisions!

Did You Ever Have to Make Up Your Mind?

Decisions come in all sizes—like cars. Some are small, compact-sized decisions, like what to eat for breakfast:
(A) Raisin Bran;
(B) Wheaties; or
(C) Spam and eggs.

Others are medium, mid-sized decisions, like what to do during summer vacation:
(A) Get a job;
(B) Go to camp; or
(C) Paint the garage.

And then there are the whopping, Lincoln Continental-sized decisions, like what to be for the rest of your life:
(A) Doctor;
(B) Lawyer;
(C) Indian Chief; or
(D) World champion hash slinger.

Small decisions confront you all the time. You face dozens of them every day, from the moment you wake up in the morning until you close your eyes at night. You decide what color socks to wear with what shirt, which TV show to watch, whether to eat an extra roll for lunch, and when to do your homework.

Medium decisions are always hovering around in the wings. They take center stage now and then to show you that there is more to life than which cereal to eat, or whether or not to wash your hair.

The big decisions loom like mountains in the

Whose Life Is It Anyway? / 9

distance, reminding you by their very presence that major issues must be confronted. Their peaks must be scaled—if not now, then soon. Very soon. By you. Alone.

Sometimes the burden of all those decisions just seems too great. You want to scream, "Hold it! Stop everything! I'm not making another decision today . . . and maybe not tomorrow, either!"

But no such luck. The world keeps moving, the decisions keep crowding in on you. There is no way out. You are stuck—along with everyone else—with making big and little choices all the rest of your life.

Actually, that statement is not quite true. A lot of people in this world try to slide by without having to make decisions at all. They want to shuffle all their responsibility off onto someone else's shoulders. And oddly enough, many people are willing to take that responsibility and tell others what to do.

Have *you* ever felt as if you would rather do anything in the world than make up your mind about something? Yet the situation demands a decision and you have to make it?

What do you do? Freeze up? Become paralyzed? Do your knees turn to jelly and your mind to mush? Would you like to pull the covers over your head and hide until the choices get tired of waiting and go away?

Think a moment. When you are confronted with having to make an important decision—which classes to take at school, for example—how does that decision make you feel? Choose one:

(A) Nervous
(B) Frustrated
(C) Anxious
(D) Happy
(E) Pessimistic
(F) Irritable

If you are like most people you did not choose (D) Happy. You probably chose one of the other words to describe how you felt. And the bigger the decision, the more nervous, frustrated, anxious, pessimistic, and irritable you become. Often there is a lot more at stake than just making yourself feel good. And unfortunately some of us wouldn't know what *would* make us happy if it crawled up and wrapped itself around our leg.

No Man Is an Island—We're All Peninsulas!

If personal happiness was all you had to consider when weighing options, making up your mind would be a snap. You would just decide what you wanted, and choose whatever came closest to making you happy at that particular point.

But usually there are others who care what you do and how you go about living your life. Your parents, family members, teachers, and that ever-changing crowd of people called your "peer group" all have a stake in how you conduct your personal affairs.

All these "watchers" exert subtle, and sometimes not-so-subtle, pressure on your decision-making process. When looking over your options you must consider not only what will make *you* happy but what will make *them* happy too. "If it is possible, as far as it depends on you, live at peace with everyone" (Romans 12:18).

But peace with *everyone* is hard to come by. For example, if the question is whether to stop dating a person you like because your parents disapprove, you could quite easily find yourself on the horns of the biggest, ripsnorting, bellowing dilemma you ever faced. The situation could come to violence (verbal or otherwise) before you make your decision, and happiness—your ultimate goal—would have flown the coop.

You have heard the saying, *No man is an island*. It's true. We are all peninsulas when it comes to making decisions, because what we do affects others.

Decision-making, a tough process to begin with, becomes even tougher when the concerns of others threaten to conflict with your personal happiness. And there are other factors that can paralyze you when you are poised on the brink of deciding.

Fear is one of them.

Blood, Sweat, and Fear

Why be afraid of making decisions? Simply because decision-making is one of the most complicated and potentially significant things a human being can do. It is plain sweat-and-blood hard work. The bigger the decision, the more anxiety it produces. There is often a great deal at stake: hopes, dreams, and ambitions of a lifetime may be riding on your ability to weigh the alternatives and arrive at a solution that works.

12 / Decisions! Decisions! Decisions!

A lot could go wrong. You could fail, choose the wrong option, or make yourself and everyone around you miserable for the rest of your life. Or you could find yourself in over your head, committing yourself beyond your ability to carry out your plans, hurting people you love. When personal expectations are high and the chance of failure is great, fear arrives like a special delivery letter bomb ready to blow up everything if you make the wrong choice.

Fear can short-circuit the decision process quicker than anything because it seems to paralyze us. Unfortunately, it isn't the only roadblock.

3-D Multiple Choice

A large number of suitable alternatives can create confusion and hinder your ability to decide. It's this simple: the more options you have, the more difficult it is to arrive at a personally satisfying decision. So you give up in frustration. You choose not to choose. The process is put on hold.

For example, 50 years ago a boy from a farming family had two choices about what to do with himself when he grew up:
(A) Follow in his father's footsteps and join the family farm; or
(B) Go to school and then join the family farm.

But times have changed. For a young person trying to decide on a career, the opportunities are endless. With all the options, decision-making becomes almost pointless. To further complicate

Whose Life Is It Anyway? / 13

matters, he may find himself training for a job that could be obsolete by the time he graduates. How can you ever hope to choose the best possible career when you don't know all the possible choices?

Remember the early days at the Burger Duke? When all they served were hamburgers, the choice was easy. Ordering went something like this:

"What'll ya have, Mack?"

"I guess I'll have a hamburger."

"Want cheese on it?"

"Yeah, thanks."

"OK. That's one burger with cheese. Here you go. Next?"

Now it's more like this:

"May we help you?"

"I guess I'll have a hamburger."

Will that be the Little Princess? The Crown Prince? The Duke? The High King? The Queen Mother?"

"Uh, the Crown Prince."

"With cheese or without?"

"Without."

"Mustard and catsup or Super Secret Sauce?"

"Oh, Super Secret Sauce."

"Pickles and onion, lettuce and tomato, or relish?"

"Umm . . . onions . . . I think. No, wait."

"No onions?"

"Right. No onions."

"Toasted bun or sesame seed bun?"

"Uh, I don't know. Just give me whatever ya got handy, ok?"

"I'm sorry, you have to choose."

"Sesame seeds sound nice. Yeah, that one."

14 / Decisions! Decisions! Decisions!

"Here or to go?"

"Here, please. Yes, I'll eat it here."

"Would you like anything to drink? We have Coke, Sprite, Dr. Pepper, orange, root beer, Pepsi, Pepsi Free, Tab, Mountain Dew, iced tea, lemonade, milk, coffee, or hot chocolate. Which would you like. . . . Hey, come back! You're not finished ordering!"

What good is it to "have it *your* way" if you aren't even sure what *your* way is?

A large number of choices makes deciding more difficult and takes more time. Many people take the easy way out and refuse to decide. They think, *A wrong decision is worse than no decision, so I will make no decision.*

Life is like a multiple-choice test in 3-D, with an infinite number of answers, of which any combination may be correct. Sometimes the mind boggles and refuses to take the test.

I Don't Care; You Decide

Too many choices can drive you crazy, but so can too few. Having the wrong kinds of alternatives can be as bad as having no alternatives at all. If you sat down in a restaurant to discover that your only choice of entrées was beef liver or pork liver, you might be likely to close the menu and say, "I guess I'm not hungry."

Obviously, if it makes no difference whether you choose Brand X over Brand Z, there can be no great incentive to choose. If the results of choosing or not choosing seem equal, why bother?

An old W.C. Fields' movie portrayed the dilemma of making a choice that didn't matter. A mother sends her young daughter to the store to buy a small item. As she was leaving, the girl asked her mother which brand she should buy. The mother says, "It makes no difference. You decide."

The daughter replies, "I don't care either. Tell me which one."

"I don't care; you decide."

"Either one, it's all the same. Tell me which one."

"You decide. I don't care."

"I don't care either; you decide."

"I don't care; you decide."

"I don't care; you decide."

This exchange goes on and on until W.C., listening from a porch swing where he's trying to take a nap, cuts the dialogue short by screaming at the girl, "I'll tell you which one, you impertinent little slip! Get along with you!"(or words to that effect).

Not deciding—or choosing not to choose—doesn't really solve anything. It only postpones the agony a little longer.

Heads I Lose; Tails I Lose

A no-win situation results when any choice you make will have a negative result. These dilemmas are far from rare. For instance, you might have found yourself in this situation: "If I skip Mary Lou's party to go out with Jim, I'll hurt Mary Lou. But if I go to the party, I'll hurt Jim."

Or, "If I don't major in premed, Dad will never speak to me again. But if I take premed, I'll never get to study electronics and be what *I* want to be."

No-win situations offer little motivation for making a choice, since they can only lead to pain and suffering—either for yourself, someone you care about, or both.

In a case of conflicting alternatives or threatening choices, you end up trying to choose the lesser of the two evils so you can weather the storm as best you can.

You're Wishy-washy, Charlie Brown!

If decision-making weren't hard enough already, there is the additional problem of self-image. We are told from the cradle to the grave that it is OK to be many things in life, but never wishy-washy.

We can be bold, determined, firm, earnest, unhesitating, and unbending. We need iron wills, steady hands, and hearts as strong as the Rock of Gibraltar. But we must never be fickle, inconsistent, drifty, double-minded, halfhearted, unresolved, timid, or unstable. No one respects people with feet of clay, knees of jelly, and shifty eyes.

To waver hesitantly between two or more alternatives is to show a weak face to the world. We all live in dread of showing weakness of any type to others. We fear the pronouncement of doom falling from the lips of our friends, "You're wishy-washy, Charlie Brown!" The burden of always trying to look like you are self-confident adds to the agony of making decisions.

The purpose of this book is to help you learn to make good decisions with confidence as you stagger under the strain of too many choices, too few choices, threatening choices, nonchallenging choices, or conflicting choices. We will examine each of these problems in future chapters. But we must begin with an even bigger issue: "What does *God* want?"

2
WHOSE LIFE IS IT ANYWAY?

Jill is one Christian teenager who has her life in order. She doesn't waver whenever she's faced with a tough choice. She enjoys the challenge of decision-making. She figures that since she has to live with her decision, she should choose whatever brings her the most satisfaction. Even so, she always considers the advice of her friends and family before finally selecting the option that seems best for her. That's as much as anyone could expect her to do, right?

Right—up to a point. But Jill, being a Christian, should consider one other opinion—God's. He is, after all, the final authority on life in general, and her life in particular.

Christians believe that God has very definite ideas about how their lives ought to be lived. But there is one monumental catch: God is not in the habit of sending telegrams to His people telling

What Does God Want? / 19

them which decision to make in any given situation. He doesn't put clues in fortune cookies or light up a crystal ball—even for the *big* decisions of life such as marriage, college, career, lifestyle, etc.

But God's indirect methods don't mean you can't find out what He wants you to do. You can. That's why *the process for making all decisions—big and little—should start with God.*

Ultimate Happiness

If we're honest, most of our decisions are based on what will make us happiest, not only in the big areas of life, but in the small ones too. For example, you choose to wear nice clothes to school because looking nice makes you feel good and feeling good makes you happy.

But personal happiness goes far deeper than just moment-by-moment pleasure. Everyone desires ultimate happiness—that feeling of gratification and fulfillment that comes from knowing who they are, where they are, and where they are going in life. This kind of ultimate happiness is actually spiritual happiness—a feeling far different from the quick self-satisfaction we are used to.

Human beings are constructed so that unless they are happy spiritually, they can never be truly happy in anything else. "For the kingdom of God is not a matter of eating and drinking, but of righteousness, peace, and joy in the Holy Spirit" (Romans 14:17).

Probably everyone knows at least one person

who looks like he has got it made—popularity, nice clothes, new car, lots of friends, and a great family. But in spite of everything he has going for him, he still isn't happy. Why?

Because, contrary to what many people think, happiness does not come from outer circumstances. Happiness grows from the inside, from that deeper self we call the spirit. If your spirit is unhappy, then nothing—not all the clothes or cars or friends or money in the world—will ever make you happy.

So, what can make your spirit happy? Simply this: choosing to do the will of God.

For Christians, true happiness lies in following Christ in *every* area of life. Here is where the importance of decision-making comes in. Sometimes Christians are called on to make decisions that would seem to go against their own wants or aims. They are asked to choose things that might be uncomfortable, or that make things harder for themselves. And they can decide to obey God if they are not after a happiness that fades—if instead they desire the true spiritual happiness that never fades.

Jesus said that to be His disciple you must pick up your cross and follow Him (Matthew 10:38). He also said that to find your life, you must lose it (John 12:25). Those are somewhat confusing images, unless you remember that Jesus is talking about spiritual life. What does it mean to carry your cross, or to lose your life in order to find it?

Ultimately, it means that all your decisions will be made with spiritual considerations in mind, and that you will seek to live out *God's* will, not just your own. It may mean passing up chances for immediate pleasure so God can work in your life to begin building spiritual happiness. Personal fulfillment and satisfaction, the deeper joys we all crave, come as a result of doing God's will. They can't be acquired in any other way.

Throw Away the Bull's-eye

Some Christians look at God's will as a series of dots that have to be connected—like those pictures you did as a kid. If all the dots are connected in the right order, you get a nice clear picture. Others see God's will as a target they have to aim for—hit the bull's-eye and win! But if they fail to hit the bull's-eye, that's it—they're finished. In other words, to some people God's will is such a narrow target that missing it puts them out of the game forever. Their lives are ruined and they can never find true happiness.

The dot-to-dot and bull's-eye methods are not the best ways to understand God's will. They tend to limit God's power by portraying Him as a demanding, short-sighted architect with a narrowly defined plan who says, "My will was for you to become a missionary doctor. You failed to take elementary chemistry in the eighth grade. I'm sorry, you're washed up." Somehow, I can't see God that way at all.

A better way to look at God's will might be in terms of a spectrum that considers what you want

22 / Decisions! Decisions! Decisions!

to do with your life, your talents and gifts, your needs, and the needs of those around you.

A spectrum offers a wide range of possibilities; it goes from one extreme to another with millions of different stages in between. So you could have an infinite number of possible options, and still be on the spectrum of God's will. The spectrum concept also suggests that wherever you are, it is possible to move one way or another to come into closer harmony with God.

This, I think, is a better way to view God's will. Forget the idea of heavenly blueprints that allow no margin for error or choice. Think instead of a living, expanding spectrum that includes an infinite variety of possibilities for your life.

A spectrum? Is that all? What does God really want? What's His ultimate goal for us?

A Heavy Gift

Some people think the question "What does God want?" is an invitation to a long, dull, theological sermon with all kinds of superspiritual-sounding words and phrases that only a seminary professor can understand. Others say, "How can ordinary teenagers know what God, the Creator of the universe and ruler of heaven, wants?" Would we understand better if we had philosophy degrees? Or an updated set of stone tablets from the mountaintop with a long list of *Thou Shalts* and *Thou Shalt Nots* to memorize?

Let's cut through those wrong assumptions

What Does God Want? / 23

right now. What God wants is very simple. *God wants us to be free.* No catch, no hidden clauses, no strings attached. He has done everything in His power to make sure we receive His incredible gift. He sent His only Son to tell us about it in person, and to die to purchase our freedom.

Jesus said that if you follow Him and believe, "You will know the truth, and the truth will set you free" (John 8:32). The Apostle Paul reminded new Christians: "It is for freedom that Christ has set us free" (Galatians 5:1). In other words, *the reason that Jesus set us free was to enjoy our freedom— not so we could become slaves to something else.* "Stand firm, then," Paul continues, "and do not let yourselves be burdened again by a yoke of slavery."

God wants us to be free to make our own decisions.

This freedom He provides is a tremendous gift (and a heavy one) which sometimes seems more of a burden than a treasure. God created the world and placed man here to rule it. Then God gave man the authority to decide how he wanted to rule (this privilege God gives is called *free will*). According to God's plan, man's decisions have real consequences—for better or worse.

You might be tempted to say, "Wait a minute, I don't feel qualified to make all my own decisions. I didn't ask for this gift of free will. I'd just as soon give it back and let God take care of things."

While everyone feels unworthy of God's gift sometimes, it is a responsibility we must learn to live with. Imagine a world in which only good and right decisions could be made. No one would have

24 / Decisions! Decisions! Decisions!

to suffer because of their own or someone else's bad decisions. If a person in this imaginary world said, "I think I'll steal this car," God would step in and say, "Oh, no you don't. That is a bad decision. I can't let you do it."

Such a world might sound good, but it is not the world we know. God has paid us the supreme compliment of allowing us to be in charge of our own affairs. He has given us power as His agents to make our own decisions, and we live by the consequences.

If God didn't give us the freedom to make a wrong decision once in a while, we might begin to think He didn't trust us. But since He does give us freedom to decide on our own, we sometimes find ourselves in tight situations where we would like to see a flashing neon sign in heaven, telling us what to do.

The Fate of Perelandra

C.S. Lewis, in his fantasy novel *Perelandra*, described a situation where a decision had to be made that would affect the future of an entire planet. Elwin Ransom, the space-traveling hero, is marooned on the planet Perelandra with the evil Dr. Weston, a madman out to destroy Perelandra by causing its sinless inhabitants to rebel against Maleldil, their creator. Ransom realizes that he is the only person who understands the consequences of such an act, and the only one who can prevent the tragedy. He faces a gigantic dilemma:

What Does God Want? / 25

whether to try to save the planet or to let the inevitable happen.

> The fate of a world really depended on how they behaved in the next few hours. The thing was irreducibly, nakedly real. They could, if they chose, decline to save the innocence of this new race, and if they declined its innocence would not be saved. It rested with no other creature in all time or all space. . . .
>
> The imprudence, the unfairness, the absurdity of it! Did Maleldil *want* to lose worlds? What was the sense of so arranging things that anything really important should finally and absolutely depend on such a man of straw as himself? . . . He writhed and ground his teeth, but could not help seeing. Thus, and not otherwise, the world was made. Either something or nothing must depend on individual choices. And if something, who could set bounds to it? (C.S. Lewis, *Perelandra*, MacMillan Co., p. 142)

In order for man to be truly free, his decisions must have real consequences—they must affect the world absolutely. If we were somehow prevented from making bad decisions, we would have no free will at all, for there would always be a wall around us. In effect, God would be saying, "This far you can go, and no farther!"

But God has set no bounds to our decisions or their consequences. We may not ever be in a position to affect the course of history for a new world. But we do, in just as crucial a way, decide

26 / Decisions! Decisions! Decisions!

our own futures in this world. For better or worse, we have the power to shape our lives by the choices we make. That, simply, is free will.

But God has not left us completely on our own to wrestle with our tough decisions. Yes, He has given us the freedom to make our own choices, but He has also promised to be around if we want to ask Him for help. So now that we've answered "What does God want?" in a general sense, we need to ask another logical question: "How can I tell what God wants me to do on a day-to-day basis?"

3
FREE TO CHOOSE, BUT NOT ALONE

Did you ever hear someone say something like, "The Lord told me I should go into full-time mission work" or "God is leading me to become more active in the church youth group"? If you're like most people, the first time you heard statements like those, you asked yourself, "How does God *lead* people? Why doesn't He tell *me* what to do?"

Maybe you're still waiting for a bass voice from the sky or a special angelic messenger with an overnight-delivery package postmarked "Heaven." If so, you may be in for a long wait. But you *can* discover God's direction through four slightly more common agents:
- the Holy Spirit,
- the Bible,
- Christian friends, and
- opportunities.

Let's examine these one at a time.

28 / Decisions! Decisions! Decisions!

Who's That Knocking on the Pipes?

Jesus promised His followers that they would not have to face the world alone. He sent His Spirit, the Holy Spirit, to comfort, lead, and strengthen them. Jesus told His disciples that, "The Counselor, the Holy Spirit, whom the Father will send in My name, will teach you all things and will remind you of everything I have said to you" (John 14:26). He also said, "You did not choose Me, but I chose you to go and bear fruit—fruit that will last." (John 15:16). Through the Holy Spirit, Jesus is with us as we go about our daily lives. He is constantly guiding and directing us—that is, as much as we will let Him.

The Holy Spirit is not a bulldozer who comes in and starts plowing up your personal landscape. He will work only in those areas where you allow Him to work. He will lead only where you allow Him to lead.

All well and good. But suppose you want to lean on the Holy Spirit's guidance in an important decision. How do you know what He wants you to do?

Good question. He doesn't write messages in the sky in the morning, or leave notes on your bathroom mirror. How do you know if the Holy Spirit is leading, or whether your own autopilot (selfish desire) is doing the flying?

A friend of mine once said that he knew when the Holy Spirit was leading him to do something because he heard Him "knocking on the pipes." What he meant was that deep down inside he could feel God's Spirit making Himself known, rattling the plumbing, and generally asserting Himself in a gentle, yet distinct, manner.

My friend's description of the guidance of the Holy Spirit is a good one. The Spirit doesn't use skywriting or personal pen notes, but an inner feeling of certainty or even distrust about the choice being considered. Here's an example:

Jean was a junior trying to decide if she should take a part-time job that would help pay for some clothes she wanted, or whether to spend that time in the drama club at school. She was offered the job, but didn't give the employer an answer right away. She had a vague feeling that the job wasn't for her.

But later she began to consider that there were other girls her age working there, and that the wages were attractive. It would be good to start a solid work record, and she could even begin to save for college. In light of those considerations, the drama club did not seem important.

So she called the employer to tell him that she would take the job. But as she dialed, something inside wouldn't let her feel right about her decision. Instead, she told the employer that she needed more time to think about it. The more she thought, though, the more she came to the conclusion that the job wasn't right for her. The clanging on her "pipes" wouldn't let her rest until she had forgotten the job and turned to her interests in the theater.

Jean's lack of peace about accepting the job is an example of how the Holy Spirit leads by a negative impulse. She couldn't feel right about her decision, and felt it was not God's will for her. But the Holy Spirit can also lead with positive direction. You may face a situation that you never dreamed you would like, and discover that you enjoy it immensely. Or find that once you commit yourself to a certain project, the nagging feeling that has been bugging you suddenly turns into a happy certainty.

The Holy Spirit directs like the rudder of a ship, guiding it first one direction and then another, pushing back and forth against the waves to give it the proper heading into the wind.

What's in the Word?

Another way God leads is through His Word, the Bible. As a collection of books, the Bible is a lot of things—poetry, history, songs, parables, eye-witness accounts of events, and much more. Through all those various types of literature runs a common thread: God's relationship with man.

The Bible shows in many ways how God has related to man through the ages. And by observing the ways in which God has moved through history, we see something of what He expects of us as individuals today. But when you use the Bible to help you make a decision, you can't just flip through the pages as you would a phone book, looking for a particular number. The "pick-and-choose" method can cause problems.

A story is told about a guy who couldn't make

up his mind what direction to take in life, so he decided to consult the Bible. He closed his eyes, opened his Bible, and let his finger drop onto a page. He read the words, "So Judas. . . . went away and hanged himself" (Matthew 27:5). Fearlessly, he turned a few more pages to try again. This time his finger dropped onto the words, "Go and do likewise" (Luke 10:37).

Many people try so hard to make the Bible work like a personal horoscope that they ignore the good guidance that it does have to offer. The Bible directs in a less flashy way, laying down principles of life that God has designed for us.

Mark and Janet had been going together for a year and were serious about continuing their relationship. Mark began to think of asking Janet to marry him. Should he or shouldn't he? He couldn't decide. Then one day a friend pointed out that the Bible cautioned against marrying non-Christians. Mark was a Christian and Janet wasn't. What should he do?

Mark looked up the passage and had his answer. God had established a biblical principle through the words of the Apostle Paul (2 Corinthians 6:14). He said that Christians should not enter into close relationships with non-Christians because the difference between them is too great. The Christian would ultimately be pulled down.

The Bible is full of down-to-earth principles for living. The Ten Commandments (Exodus 20) form a basic blueprint of what God expects His people to do. Jesus' Sermon on the Mount gave further application for God's 10 basic principles. (The Sermon on the Mount is found in Matthew 5–7, and is considered to be the heart of Christ's teaching.)

Biblical guidance is more than a list of do's and don'ts for Christians. The Bible is very specific on many issues, but it is also a guidebook which opens the reader's eyes to danger areas on the road ahead and offers help to steer him away from problems. It points out improper attitudes and directs the reader toward a better understanding of life.

The best reason I know to study the Bible is to help develop your "spiritual eyesight" so you can see clearly where you are going. The more knowledge you have of biblical principles, the easier it will be for you to make decisions.

Anyone wondering whether it's OK to have sex before marriage, for example, already has an answer. The Bible is specific on that issue. Paul says that among Christians, "there must not be even a hint of sexual immorality, or of any kind of impurity, or of greed, because these are improper for God's holy people" (Ephesians 5:3). So it really isn't worth agonizing over—the decision has already been made for you.

You might say, "If the decision has been taken out of the Christian's hands regarding premarital sex, then he isn't free at all."

A basic misconception about freedom and free will is that *freedom* means a complete absence of discipline. Not true. While there may be no boundaries to the power of our free will, we have the basic responsibility to use our power of choice wisely. Without principles for everyone to follow,

Free To Choose, but Not Alone / 33

freedom quickly degenerates into chaos.

For instance, if highways had no traffic signs and no patrolmen, driving would be a take-your-life-in-your-hands challenge. But with rules of the road, people can get where they're going quite easily. The rules do not infringe on the freedom of the driver to go where he chooses. He is still free. (He's even free to break the rules and face the penalty for doing so.)

The Bible teaches us to be disciplined so that we may be completely free. Paul tells us that, "All Scripture is God-breathed and is useful for teaching, rebuking, correcting, and training in righteousness" (2 Timothy 3:16). It never seeks to cripple us by forcing us into straitjackets of conformity, even though many sincere people seem to prefer rules to follow rather than freedom to enjoy. God wants you to use your free will wisely as He gives you advice through His Word.

A Little Help from My Friends

A third way God guides is through other Christians. He expects us to help one another work out our struggles and decisions in life. He has given us the fellowship of other believers to serve as a means of encouragement and support, "That you and I may be mutually encouraged by each other's faith" (Romans 1:12).

Many young people needlessly drag around enormous burdens, worrying about what to do and forgetting that others have gone through exactly the same situation (and even lived to tell about it)! When you need help facing a decision or are struggling with a problem, the answer will often come when you share your need with a Christian friend.

God provides guidance through the advice and concern of other Christians. Sometimes the personal importance of the decision blocks out what God wants to tell us. Another Christian, free from the emotional burden of the problem, can hear more clearly what God is saying.

When Opportunity Knocks

God also guides through a fourth method—the circumstances of our lives. It only makes sense to expect God to use the opportunities that come to us to give us direction.

Suppose you believed that God wanted you to do something special. Wouldn't it stand to reason that He would make a way for you to do it? When He wanted His people out of Egypt, He didn't let the Red Sea stop them!

In the same way, if God is directing you toward a college education or a job in a specific field, you can be sure that He will give you an opportunity to follow His direction.

Many people talk of open and closed doors when they speak of God's will. He sometimes seems to guide us by opening some doors and closing others. It is not unusual for someone who has just made a big decision to look back and say,

"I had so many different options that I just didn't know which one to choose. But when I finally had to make a decision, all but one had closed to me. That's the one I picked and I've never been happier."

If God's methods sound a little supernatural, they are. But any Christian who places his life in God's hands and trusts Him to lead can expect to receive clear guidance.

Did you notice the "catch" in the sentence above? God provides His Holy Spirit, His Word (the Bible), Christian counselors, and well-placed opportunities to guide us along the spectrum of His will. But these four influences won't help us much if we don't *trust* God.

Whom Do You Trust?

In the last chapter we saw how God loves and trusts us enough to let us make all our own decisions and be entirely free. Just because He offers four forms of guidance doesn't mean He doesn't trust us. He just knows we're likely to need help with many of our big (and little) decisions. The question is whether or not we trust God enough to follow the advice He offers.

Some people are hesitant to put their trust in God. They think, *If I put my life in God's hands, He'll make me a missionary to Iran! I'll be miserable for the rest of my life!* Something in all of us fears opening up to God completely because of our "old fogy" image of Him standing over us and saying, "I'm going to make you a worthwhile person if it kills you."

Remember this: *God loves you.* In fact, Jesus loved you so much that He willingly took your place of execution and died for you. Would Anyone who loves you that much want to ruin your life by forcing you to do something you hate? If you can't trust Someone with that much love for you, whom *can* you trust?

God knows us better than we know ourselves. He knows our strengths and our weaknesses. He knows what will ultimately make us happy. He will give us the desires of our hearts (Psalm 37:4), and can make our lives richer and fuller and happier than we could ever manage on our own.

When you approach a choice in life, you can be sure that God will give you wisdom during the decision-making process (James 1:5). He does not stand off somewhere watching to see what you will choose. He stands beside you, leading, guiding, knocking on the pipes now and then, and pointing out the way to go. He directs as a friend would, because ultimately the choice is yours. He won't veto your decision because you are free to choose. But you will never have to make your tough decisions alone.

4
WHEN DECISIONS GO BAD

Bill decides to enlist in the army because he says it will "make a man of him." A year later he is sending tear-stained letters home telling his family how terribly lonely he feels.

Karen decides to cut her beautiful long hair in order to wear one of the newer, shorter styles. The next day she refuses to go to school because she can't face her friends looking "like a boy."

Allen decides he would like to "settle down" and date only one girl. A few months after he does, he finds himself bored and frustrated with the relationship, but he can't bring himself to break it off because it would hurt his girlfriend.

Nancy decides to drive her brother's car to a friend's house. On the way home she discovers a small dent that wasn't there before. She feels terrible and apologizes, but now her brother won't let her borrow anything of his.

Judy decides to go to a two-year nursing school instead of the college where most of her friends are. At the end of the first year all she can think of is the fun she could have had. But she has invested too much in the nursing program to drop out now.

Greg decides one night that drinking a few beers with his friends won't hurt anything. On the way home he runs into a parked car belonging to the neighbors. If he reports the accident, his insurance will be suspended, so his parents agree to pay the damages. But Greg has to pay them back, and is grounded until the bill is settled.

Have you ever made any decisions that backfired? Of course, everyone has. Even choices that seem great at the time can sometimes go bad, and all you can mutter is, "It wasn't supposed to turn out this way. What happened?"

Almost all bad decisions result from the same problem: the normal decision-making process gets short-circuited.

If you've ever had to deal with the outcome of a bad judgment, chances are it was because the decision-making process at some point was, as we say in the decision business, "trashed."

"Ah!" you say. "You mean there is a specific process that everyone can follow?"

Right! Aware of it or not, you go through the procedure all the time—we all do. Everyone goes through the same process, whether the choice is to wear shoes or go barefoot, buy a Chevy or buy a Ford, get married or join the marines. It doesn't matter how big or trivial the decision is, we all go through the same process every time. But if any step is skipped, it spells T-R-O-U-B-L-E.

Five Easy Pieces

Making a decision is a rational act. When faced with a choice between two or more alternatives, a challenge, or a threat which requires action, right away the brain zips into action.

For example, if you were walking in the woods and suddenly a huge bear jumped out from the bushes and started toward you with a hungry gleam in his beady brown eyes, most likely your feet would start moving in the other direction with no thought at all. You would not be aware that five important steps had just taken place. But your brain would.

In an instant, your brain would have raced through the five steps of decision-making in record time—the same steps it uses when you try to decide what kind of deodorant to buy.

Here they are:
1. *Sizing up the situation*
2. *Examining the options*
3. *Weighing the options*
4. *Thinking the plan through*
5. *Putting the decision into effect*

(A sixth step, evaluation, will be discussed in chapter 11.)

40 / Decisions! Decisions! Decisions!

Using the bear-in-the-woods example, let's see how each step works.

Step #1—Sizing Up the Situation

When Brer Bear leaps out onto the trail ahead, his presence presents a challenge—to life, liberty, and the continued pursuit of happiness. In sizing up the situation, your brain will ask questions like, *Do bears eat meat? How fast can they run? Do they have good eyesight? Do they bluff easily?* and other questions which help to define the nature of the challenge. As the answers pour in, based on your knowledge of bears, you will decide that the situation definitely warrants some kind of action. And on you go to:

Step #2—Examining the Options

So, action is necessary. What choices come to mind? Hiding in the middle of a large city? Climbing a nearby tree? Jumping in the lake? Running in the opposite direction? Explaining to the bear why you wouldn't make a decent lunch? Getting tough? Fighting it out? All are possible alternatives. And so, on to:

Step #3—Weighing the Options

Once your options have been nailed down, it's time to weigh them to see which one offers the best chance of reaching your goal: survival. Hiding in a large city would certainly be effective, but there's probably not a large city in the middle of your woods. Climbing a nearby tree is a possibility, but a quick glance shows that there are no large trees nearby. Jumping in the lake is probably not the best solution, since you've heard that bears are fond of water and have been known to wash their food before eating it. Explaining to the bear is risky since he may see things quite differently than you do. Fighting it out is chancy since the bear outweighs you by about 900 pounds and has a definite "reach" advantage.

So you are left with the choice of running away, which has some attractive merits—it's cheap, easy to do, effective, and leaves room for other choices should they arise. So your brain moves on to:

Step #4—Thinking the Plan Through

Once you find a suitable option, your mind steps back a little to project the possible outcome if that solution is used. It asks, *Can I live with this decision? Will others think I am foolish? Is this right for me?* Answers immediately flood in, reassuring you that, yes, running away is a decision you can live with. It is one that is not foolish in the least, and therefore, right for you. Which brings up:

Step #5—Putting the Decision into Effect

The chosen option must be put into effect at once. Your brain, delighted with its choice, sends out a direct command to the locomotion department and gives the order for one fast getaway: *Feet, get moving!* And away you go.

A decision has been made and acted on. The operation was a success.

Blowing It

If every choice were as simple as what to do when a bear makes a lunch date with you, decision-making would be a snap. Unfortunately, only a

42 / Decisions! Decisions! Decisions!

handful of life's dilemmas are that simple. Most are complicated with layers of tangled emotions, expectations, and human weaknesses. Sometimes those problems are enough to throw the decision-making process into a malfunction mode.

Whenever you reach the point of no return in a decision, look back, and say, "Boy, I really blew it!" chances are it is because the decision-making process did not glide smoothly through the five steps. Some problem in your mental computer scrambled the program and out popped a bad decision. It can happen any time one or more of the five steps is skipped.

John had been having trouble with his parents. He had been getting into a lot of arguments and began to feel that they didn't want him around. So, after a really bad fight with his dad one night, he left home and started hitchhiking to the West Coast. He didn't get very far when police in another city charged him with vagrancy (wandering with no home or means of support) and called his parents.

In John's case, it's easy to see what went wrong. When confronted with the choice of staying home and working out his problems with his parents, he failed to examine and weigh the options. He didn't stop to think the plan through. He skipped steps two, three, and four, and went directly to putting his decision into effect—with disastrous results for himself and everyone involved.

Karen couldn't decide whether to take American History or Civics. She liked American History but was afraid that she wouldn't know anyone in that

When Decisions Go Bad / 43

class all because her friends were taking Civics at the same hour. When her friends asked her to take Civics with them, she agreed on the spot. A month later she was barely making a passing grade because she was so bored and miserable.

Karen probably failed to size up the situation correctly. When she examined and weighed the options, the choices seemed fuzzy and she was easily swayed by her friends. She skipped step four and did not think her plan through. She ended up struggling in a class she hated when she would probably have enjoyed and aced the other class.

The Heart of the Matter

Examples of short-circuited decision-making like John's and Karen's can be found by the dozens. It's too bad, because decision-making doesn't have to have bad results. The most common mistake is that the decision-maker lets his heart rule his head. In a moment of hot temper or confusion, the decision is made before the head can logically sort out the information and come up with the best solution.

Too often bad decisions result from acting on our "gut reactions" rather than considering the best possible information. It might sound like this emphasis on rational decisions contradicts what we have said about the emotionally oriented leading of the Holy Spirit (knocking on the pipes). It really doesn't.

44 / Decisions! Decisions! Decisions!

Acting on hunches, moments of emotional stress, or casual flip-of-the-coin carelessness is not at all helpful to the work of the Holy Spirit. Making a decision because it "feels" right or good, or because you believe God is leading you a certain way is no excuse for skipping any of the five steps.

The Holy Spirit does not short-circuit the rational decision-making process with an emotional override. He works *within* the process to bring you to the best result. If I had to pin down the point where God most directly influences the decision-making process, I would say Step 4—thinking the plan through—even though He guides us along each step of the process if we let Him.

When we actually begin to think the plan through, God through the Holy Spirit can best direct us. Step 4 involves looking ahead and trying to imagine yourself in future circumstances.

God, since He is master of the future, can help you see what the consequences might be in each situation. The picture He creates for you then enters into your decision-making process. Sometimes there will be an emotional jolt that goes along with a certain future image. The proposed decision might feel right or wrong, and you can either go ahead with it or go back to Step 2 and examine other options.

If It Feels Good . . .

God gets blamed for a lot of bad outcomes because we often assume that because we get an emotional tingle, it is His way of leading us. You have probably had heard someone say, "I know this is what God wants me to do because it feels so right." Or, "God wouldn't let me do anything not in His will for me, so I know it's right."

Neither of these attitudes is valid when it comes to making wise decisions. Good feelings are not positive evidence of anything except that you feel good. Many horrible situations started out with great happiness—and ignorance.

Believing that God would not let you do anything that wasn't in His will for you is a basic deterministic attitude (whatever will be, will be). But since God has trusted man with free will, He cannot very well prevent you from doing something out of His will. God will *not* make you into a preprogrammed robot. He will let you do whatever you please, even if it's wrong.

Emotions can short-circuit the decision-making process quicker than anything, causing you to skip the vital step-by-step procedure. When you are upset, grouchy, nervous, excited, disturbed, or even happy and optimistic, you need to be on guard. Strong feelings have a way of clouding issues and demanding snap decisions in which one or more necessary steps are skipped.

We don't have to be cold, relentlessly logical, unfeeling drones. Some of our decisions—such as who to marry—will be filled with emotional content. No one ever completely divorces his emotions from his logical self. But we should try to balance the emotional aspect of decision-making with solid, rational thought. We need the perspective that our good commonsense mental abilities can bring.

Mind Control

The main thing to remember is that decision-making is an active mental process, never a passive one. The words used to describe the five steps should give us a clue here: *sizing up, examining, weighing, thinking,* and *putting into effect.* These words describe active tasks which the decider must tackle aggressively. Since decision-making is a mental exercise, primarily under the control of the mind, it can be examined, broken down into parts, analyzed, organized, and standardized.

If the process sounds a little too complicated, it really isn't. You do these same things in countless ways every minute of the day. God has given you the world's most advanced computer—your brain—to help you in your decision-making.

What is more, He has promised that He will help. "If any of you lacks wisdom, he should ask God, who gives generously to all without finding fault, and it will be given to him" (James 1:5). That's good news. If you have never asked God for wisdom, it would be a good idea to ask Him now. He will give you guidance so you can begin to make better decisions.

Good decision-makers know what they are doing when they make a choice. They know each step of the process and can guide themselves through it, reaching the end with confidence in

When Decisions Go Bad / 47

themselves and in the decision they have made.

The following chapters describe the step-by-step process in more detail, so you can use it to start making better decisions right away.

5
ASKING THE RIGHT QUESTIONS

A word in computer language sums up where most of us go wrong in making decisions: *GIGO*. The word is short for *Garbage In, Garbage Out*. Translated into everyday speech, it simply means that the answer you get from a computer is only as good as the information put into it. If you put errors into the system, you get errors back.

Happily, the opposite is also true. If you use correct information you get good, solid answers. Any computer is only as reliable as its program.

The brain is the most powerful and creative computer the world has ever known. Not even the largest, most sophisticated electronic machines can come close to doing what your mind can do with ease. After all, there's only so much you can do with a silicon chip. Brain potential is unlimited.

But just like a computer, your brain can only produce good decisions if the information you give it is good. Often, when a bad decision is made, it is because the input was faulty in some way.

Debugging Your Brain

What we need is a device for debugging the brain—getting out all the nasty little errors that can throw a glitch into the system. Computer programmers call these errors *bugs*, but whatever you call them they're a nuisance. If a programmer discovers a glitch in the program, he goes after the bug that produced it. Usually, he'll start at the very beginning. That's where we need to start too.

Step one of the decision-making process begins when you suddenly become aware that a decision must be made. This happens, for example, when you go to your closet in the morning looking for something to wear and discover that there is a whole rack of shirts and sweaters, any one of which will do the job. But which one should you choose?

You note the situation, and right away you begin to size it up. Are you going to school? To your cousin's wedding? To clean the basement? A whole new set of questions would have to be considered in each case to find the right thing to wear. If you just reached into your closet and put on the first thing you grabbed, you could end up standing around your cousin's wedding reception wearing a Pac-Man T-shirt.

Even small matters, such as what to wear or what to have for lunch, are influenced by how we

50 / Decisions! Decisions! Decisions!

size up the situation. The big decisions depend even more on a correct evaluation of the situation. But often we insist on letting our emotions sidetrack the big decisions of life. When we do, the sizing-up process gets off and running on the wrong track.

Judy had been going with Mike for about six months when she discovered he was developing a pretty heavy drinking problem. Since he never drank around her parents she tried to ignore it. But soon she began to worry about riding in the car with him after he had been drinking. The situation continued until she felt a decision had to be made.

But what should she do? She asked herself, *Should I tell him to stop, break up with him, make him get help for his problem, refer him to Alateen, ignore his drinking, or what?*

Judy couldn't decide because she wasn't receiving clear emotional leading for any of the choices. She feared losing Mike and didn't want to break up with him. But she also feared getting in a car accident if his drinking continued. The two fears seemed equally bad and she felt helpless to make any definite decision.

The Art of Asking

Question: Getting the right answer is all that counts. True or False?

Answer: False.

People tend to think that in any question-and-answer situation getting the right answer is all that

Asking the Right Questions / 51

is important. That might be true for tests, but not for decision-making, because the kind of question you ask is just as important as the answer. In fact, if you don't ask the right questions, you will never get the right answer.

The art of asking questions is easy to learn. You might say it is all a matter of phrasing—not so much *what* you say as *how* you say it. But before we look at the proper ways of asking a decision question, let's look at some common errors decision-makers commit.

The Multiple-choice Question

Judy, in the previous example, asked a multiple-choice question when she thought, *Should I tell him to stop, break up with him, make him get help for his problem, refer him to Alateen, ignore his drinking, or what?*

What she was doing was putting all her choices into the question at once where they quickly got tangled together. With so many issues expressed at once, it became impossible for her to decide between them. The multiple-choice question destroyed her decision process before it could even get started.

The No-win Question

Sometimes we ask ourselves questions that make us feel like instant losers. There's no way to win.

52 / Decisions! Decisions! Decisions!

Usually, these questions pose two alternatives which would have equally disturbing results.

Should I ask the teacher for an extra day on this assignment and get yelled at or should I just hand it in and take an F? Or, *Should I go to the beach with my friends and miss the big game, or should I watch the game and miss all the fun at the beach?*

The Gut-wrencher Question

Many people are fond of asking emotionally charged questions that pack a wallop and really start the adrenalin flowing. Usually these questions take forms such as, *Should I keep dating Nancy, who says she would fall apart without me, even though I'm miserable when we're together?*

Obviously, this kind of question increases the likelihood of a "gut reaction" rather than a logical approach to the situation.

The Trick Question

The danger of trick questions is that they come packaged with the proper response. For instance, *Isn't it foolish for me to spend four years in college when I could be getting valuable work experience in a very competitive job market?* The answer is, "Yes, of course."

But the same question could also be asked this way: *Wouldn't it be better for me to go to college and learn as much as I can about myself before committing myself to a career that might not satisfy me in a couple of years?* The answer again is, "Yes, of course."

So nothing was actually decided because each question implied its own answer and did not leave room for rational discussion.

Garbage-free Questions

Good decision-making questions are garbage-free. They strip away the clutter and get right to the heart of the matter. They do not offer unlimited choices, force you into a no-win situation, get your stomach churning, or play psychological games.

So after you complete Step #1, sizing up the situation, you need to ask yourself, *What should I do?* "Should I" questions work best for making decisions, because they meet all the criteria we have discussed. They are:
- simple
- neutral
- limited in scope
- structured for maximum input

Let's examine each of these criteria separately.

Simple—"Should I" questions can be made simple if we refuse to load them down with options. We won't turn them into multiple-choice problems if we limit the question to one specific alternative.

Neutral—A "Should I" question is emotionally neutral. It doesn't take sides or evaluate. It simply offers the option of doing or not doing something. By its very nature it leads the decision-maker to the next logical step: examining the options.

Limited in scope—A good "Should I" question resists the temptation to examine the whole complex issue at once. Instead, it focuses on only one narrow objective: to obtain information for dealing with the specific problem at hand. The situation may touch on many issues and have far-reaching results, but the individual questions never should.

Structured for maximum input—Good "Should I" questions do not come with prepackaged answers, but they do invite additional input and information to further the decision-making process. They encourage discussion and allow cases to be made for all options, so the decision-maker has some control over the outcome. Asked properly, they encourage consideration of every option, rather than confusing the issue with emotionally charged, no-win, or trick solutions.

The goal of the "Should I" question is to frame the situation so that as many options as possible can be considered. A good decision-maker can move from step one to step two without carrying along a lot of excess baggage if he asks the right questions.

Let's take another look at the problem-causing questions to see if we can rephrase them into problem-solvers.

Problem-causer #1: "Should I tell my boyfriend to stop drinking, break up with him, make him get help for his problem, refer him to Alateen, ignore his drinking, or what?"

Problem-solver #1: "Should I break up with my boyfriend?" This question is simple, direct, and

Asking the Right Questions / 55

cuts out a lot of the issues that aren't as important as the main one. After the primary question is answered yes or no, the secondary issues can then be dealt with.

Problem-causer #2: "Should I go to the beach with my friends and miss the big game, or should I watch the game and miss all the fun at the beach?"

Problem-solver #2: "Should I go to the beach?" You can avoid the pain of a no-win question if you simply limit yourself to the problem at hand (whether or not to go to the beach). Then you are free to explore options for and against going to the beach without commenting on the outcome either way.

Problem-causer #3: "Should I keep dating Nancy, who says she would fall apart without me, even though I'm miserable when we're together?"

Problem-solver #3: "Should I keep dating Nancy?" Stripping away all the emotional baggage is the only good way to deal with a gut-wrenching question. Then decisions can be made without the pressure of heavy dramatics.

Problem-causer #4: "Isn't it foolish for me to spend four years in college when I could be getting valuable work experience in a very competitive job market?"

Problem-solver #4: "Should I go to college?" Trick questions that come with their own answers stifle all serious input. You can avoid these questions if you stick to defining the basic situation at hand.

56 / Decisions! Decisions! Decisions!

Then you can begin exploring all options objectively.

Can you see the advantage of "Should I" questions that require simple, direct answers? From there you can build cases for or against doing what the question suggests.

Breaking the Bad Habit

If you are in the habit of asking decision questions in the wrong way, it may take some practice to get the hang of it. But once you learn how, it's easy. The good thing about decision questions is that you can stop and take a look at them to see if you have put them into the right form. It's a good idea to write them down on paper.

Here are a few questions that could be phrased more effectively to help speed the decision-making process along. For practice, grab a pen and paper and rephrase each question so it will solve problems instead of causing additional ones.

1. "Wouldn't it be better to sleep in on Saturday morning instead of going to band practice?"

2. "Should I take a study period, try to get into that new art class, or ask for an independent study in English or History?"

3. "Should I tell Bill that Jean is mad at him so that he can apologize, or should I stay out of it and let him find out for himself—even though his friendship with Jean might be destroyed?"

4. "Should I ask Mary Ann to go out next Saturday night and let her turn me down, or should I

forget it and stay home again like I usually do?"

5. "Would it be better to help Dad clean out the garage, like I promised, or to fix my car so I won't be late for school anymore?"

There is no single "correct" way to rephrase any of these questions. They can be corrected or revised in many different ways. But you know you did it right if you made your questions simple, neutral, limited in scope, and structured for maximum input. Look them over again and see if you followed the four rules for phrasing decision questions. Samples of revised questions are on page 59.

Walking by Faith

Analyzing your decision questions may seem awkward and artificial at first. You may even suspect that the process gets in the way of spiritual growth. Perhaps you feel that all this self-examination indicates a lack of trust in God.

These are valid issues. However, the purpose of the method we are exploring in this book is not to diminish God's interaction in the events and decisions of your life. Instead, it is to get you to open your eyes to what you are doing, break harmful bad decision-making habits, and replace them with good ones.

You are not showing a lack of faith if you carefully weigh the challenge before you and analyze the questions you are asking. Actually, you are putting yourself in a better position to let God work with

58 / Decisions! Decisions! Decisions!

you and through you. God says, "I will instruct you and teach you in the way you should go; I will counsel you and watch over you" (Psalm 32:8).

It is well worth the effort to analyze, to struggle to make good rational decisions, and to take responsibility and control for your life.

In the Bible, God is often associated with wisdom and knowledge. God's Spirit is described as "the Spirit of wisdom and of understanding, the Spirit of counsel and of power, the Spirit of knowledge" (Isaiah 11:2). He is a reasoning Being, as we are. And He is pleased when we use our minds to better understand and examine what we are doing and why.

To walk by faith does not mean you blindly fumble through life with your brain switched off. It means you go wide-eyed, alert, and conscious of what you are doing and where you are going every step of the way.

Hopefully, you can now take the first step—sizing up the situation by asking the right questions. Spend a few minutes now sizing up the situations in your own life. What questions do you need to ask? Have them clearly in mind before you continue. When you're ready to take another step, read on.

Asking the Right Questions / 59

Here's one way you might have rephrased the questions on pages 56-57.
1. "Should I go to band practice?"
2. "Should I try to get into the new art class?"
3. "Should I tell Bill that Jean is mad at him?"
4. "Should I ask Mary Ann to go out?"
5. "Should I help Dad clean out the garage?"

6
A MATTER OF CHOICE

I once worked with a surveying crew. It was an interesting job—a little like treasure-hunting. Every morning we would drive to some spot in the country, take out all our equipment, and spend the whole day tramping around the woods, fields, and farms. The basic idea was to take a look at the land, find out what was there, and write it down.

We used the information we gathered to make maps. Someone would call the surveyor's office to request a survey of his land, and we would go take a look. We used various means of measuring in order to be as accurate as possible so a good map could be made.

The surveying process is similar to what happens when you are trying to make up your mind. In Step #1—sizing up the situation—you are faced with a challenge that requires action (the call to the surveyor's office). In Step #2—examining the options—you take a look around to gather any information you can find.

Those Nasty Roadblocks

Examining (surveying) options may be simple, but it is also a process easily wrecked. Several nasty roadblocks can halt forward progress:
- Too many choices
- Not enough choices
- Threatening choices
- Nonchallenging choices
- Conflicting choices

These roadblocks were mentioned in chapter 1, but let's take a closer look at each one in light of what we have learned so far.

Too Many Choices—Ed had a free Saturday when he didn't have to work. He had looked forward to it all week, and when the day finally arrived he wanted to make the most of it. As he sat down and tried to figure out what to do, he thought of dozens of things right away: go to the beach, read a book, go to a movie, go fishing, play ball with some friends, go over to Heather's, take a nap, watch TV, take his little brother to the park. . . . As the list grew longer, Ed became more discouraged and frustrated. Which was the best option? How could he ever decide between them?

Problems result from having too many choices. The decision-making computer becomes crammed with an avalanche of options, the circuits overload, and fuses start to blow.

62 / Decisions! Decisions! Decisions!

Not Enough Choices—Megan was looking for a new pair of shoes for school. She had looked in several stores but couldn't find any she liked. Finally, at the last store in the mall she found a pair that came *close* to the style she had in mind, but they were $10 more than she wanted to spend. She couldn't decide what to do—go ahead and spend the extra money for something that wasn't exactly what she wanted, or keep looking even though her choices seemed slim.

Megan couldn't make up her mind because her inner decision-making computer just did not have enough suitable choices to process. As a result, it creaked to a halt.

Threatening Choices—Kyle borrowed his dad's car to go to the store without asking. When he came out, one of the taillights had been smashed by a careless driver. He then had a tough decision to make. Should he tell his dad about the accident and lose the privilege of driving the family car? Or take the afternoon off from work to get it fixed, and risk losing his part-time job?

Kyle couldn't decide. Both options made him look bad. Either way he looked at it, he was doomed. The choices were too threatening.

Nonchallenging Choices—Anne was asked to pick out the colors for new choir robes. There were three options: red and white, blue and white, or gold and white. She was told that any of the colors would be OK, and that she should just pick whichever she liked.

At that point Anne couldn't decide. All the color

combinations looked good to her. Anyway, what difference did it make? Her decision-making device stalled as she thought, *This is beneath me. Flip a coin if you want to, but I won't be bothered with anything this trivial.*

Conflicting Choices—Jack had planned to go to a large college near his hometown with most of his friends. But then he was offered an academic scholarship to a smaller school several hundred miles away. If he chose the big school he would be near his family and friends, but he would have to work long hours to afford tuition. If he took the scholarship he would have more time to study, but he would be far from home where he didn't know anybody.

Getting Back on Track

If your decision process ever stops after you have examined your options, you have probably run smack up against one of these blockades. If so, step back and see if you can identify exactly what the problem is. Once you are able to recognize what kind of roadblock you are facing, you will be in a better position to navigate around it and get back on the right track.

You may need new information. Remember *GIGO* (garbage in, garbage out)? Make sure your facts are straight. But computers can also fail to function because of "insufficient data." Maybe you can't make your decision because you don't have enough information to go on.

What do you need to know to get things running again? Should you read the newspapers? Check out the encyclopedias? Go to Summer School? Write to Ann Landers?

None of the above! What you need to get past a decision blockade is to enlarge the scope of your choices. In other words, include more details in your survey and increase your options. How? By *brainstorming*.

Care and Feeding of a Brainstorm

Brainstorming is sitting down by yourself (or with a group of other people) and writing down every idea that comes into your head(s). And even though it is a delicate art that takes a special knack, it's also a lot of fun to do.

All you need for successful brainstorming is a quiet place where you can concentrate, a pad and pencil, and a little time. The idea is to just let your mind go where it will while you write down the thoughts that come to you—no matter how strange they may seem.

Suppose you were trying to decide what to do with a free Saturday afternoon. If all you could think of was to go swimming or stay home, perhaps neither choice would appeal to you very much. But if you were to begin brainstorming, you could come up with dozens more options in very little time. After five minutes your sheet of paper might look like this:

A Matter Of Choice / 65

Ways to spend Saturday afternoon:

go fly a kite	go to the zoo
run for governor	start a garden
fly to the moon	roller-skate
read a book	make fudge
write a book	make a cake
go to the library	enroll in night school
make friends with the neighbors	teach the dog a new trick
clean the garage	set up a terrarium
paint a picture	build an ant farm
take some pictures	start a bug collection
frame some photographs	go on a nature walk

Read through the list again to see all the different things that brainstorming brought out. Some are frivolous (run for governor, fly to the moon), some are probably too ambitious for one afternoon (write a book, enroll in night school), and some are actually good ideas (go to the library, frame some photographs).

One idea suggests another. Ideas have hooks on them—one always pulls another out with it. They build on one another and the list grows. So something that appears to be ridiculous might lead to something worthwhile.

That's the secret of good brainstorming: allowing the ideas to flow and just writing them down as they come. Soon you have a chain reaction of all kinds of ideas. And out of those ideas will come one that will work.

66 / Decisions! Decisions! Decisions!

Brainstorming is an excellent way to unlock your creativity, using it to help remove the roadblock. As you play with the problem and let all sorts of possible solutions bubble up from your brain, you will eventually hit on something that you never would have thought about otherwise.

In fact, some large corporations are so convinced that brainstorming helps their overall productivity that they schedule regular sessions for their personnel. This powerful tool is turned loose on corporate problems, and used to generate new ideas for products and research. Some of the best ideas in the world were born out of brainstorming sessions.

Like anything of a creative nature, there are certain rules to follow when brainstorming so you won't stifle creativity. The #1 rule is this: *Do not criticize.* Reserve judgment until later.

Nothing stops brainstorming quicker than a negative attitude or comment. You are to mine the raw material that will be sifted later for gems. Almost everyone has been in a situation where ideas were flying fast and furious in a spontaneous brainstorming session. The mood is light and fun, and the creativity is rolling along. Then someone says, "That's the stupidest idea I ever heard!"

Bam! The fun is over and the brainstorming session collapses like a tent with its center pole yanked out. Ideas dry up and the flow evaporates. Negative comments like, "That's dumb," or "It'll never work," kill brainstorming and shut off the idea-generating power.

Because we are not used to playing around with

A Matter of Choice / 67

ideas, it is very hard to let them just flow without making some kind of comment. We automatically want to judge them. But good brainstormers have learned to open the creative gates, let the ideas flow freely, and reserve judgment until later.

With practice you can get the knack. It can be done alone or with others to good effect. Once you have all the ideas on paper, you can begin to evaluate and sort out the options that offer help from the ones that don't.

So What?

"That's great about brainstorming," you say, "but so what? How does it help me when I'm trying to decide which school to go to, or what kind of career to enter?"

Brainstorming is a lever. It's a valuable tool for all decision-makers. The common denominator for decision-stalling roadblocks is the lack of *acceptable* options. So brainstorming can help you come up with more good choices and move the process on to the next step.

You may doubt the need for brainstorming when faced with too many choices. However, what you see as "too many choices" often is "too few good choices" or "nonchallenging choices." In other words, you may have a lot of options, but not the right ones for you. Brainstorming *will* help get the ball rolling in a different direction—one that will take you where you want to go.

Even if the problem is threatening choices or

conflicting choices, brainstorming works the same way. By listing new options, you clear your mental logjam by clarifying or adding to the choices already under consideration.

Parents and friends can help too. If you run low on ideas, ask others for helpful alternatives. But be careful. Don't ask for advice: "What do you think I should do?" Instead, get input: "Can you help me think of some things I might try?" It is better to reduce the unwanted emotional content of the answer and not ask them to decide for you. You want options that will help *you* decide.

Making a Case

Coming to a decision is like arguing a case in court. Any good lawyer knows that he doesn't dare go to court unless he knows every detail of what happened, why, how, and when. Only then can he present his client in the best light. His job is to represent his client, but he could argue the case from either side. It is *not* a lawyer's job to get emotionally involved in the case. He concentrates solely on getting the facts and presenting them as clearly and persuasively as possible. He then lets the judge and jury evaluate the information and decide guilt or innocence.

The same method holds true for good decision-making. You must separate yourself from the emotional detours of the case and concentrate instead on gathering the facts, presenting them clearly, and evaluating them fairly. Decision-making is, as we have stressed, primarily a logical process. The best way to handle it is like a lawyer presenting a case.

Spiritual Considerations

One area a Christian must never overlook when stating his case is the somewhat fuzzy realm of spiritual considerations. These stand out from other facts because they contain distinct moral viewpoints.

Spiritual considerations might arise *directly from a Bible commandment*, such as "You shall not steal" (Exodus 20:15), or "Love your neighbor as yourself" (Mark 12:31). They might also arise *from general principles or examples in the Bible*, such as putting God's will above ours (Luke 22:42), or going the second mile for someone (Matthew 5:41). A spiritual consideration might also be recognized *in a personal way* by applying what you know of Christ's values to your own situation.

Spiritual considerations are those moral or ethical standards that separate Christians from non-Christians in their approach to life, and bring a unique dimension to the decision-making process for Christians.

For example, in trying to decide whether to get married, it probably wouldn't matter to a non-Christian whether or not his future mate was a Christian. But such a consideration would be crucial for a Christian because it involves a spiritual principle (see 2 Corinthians 6:14).

Spiritual considerations are learned through Bible study and growth in faith. As you try to focus on the various aspects of a decision, the Holy Spirit may bring spiritual considerations to mind. Of course, not every decision you face (such as which car to buy, or whether to go to the beach) will involve a spiritual consideration.

But it might! That's why *Christians should always examine their decisions from Christ's point of view so they don't overlook what might be important.* In making a case for or against whatever situation you are examining, you may discover a factor which has special meaning to you as a Christian. If so, just write it down with all the other facts. A consideration does not decide a case one way or another. It is just one more point to be weighed when you make your decision.

Later we will examine in greater detail how to address these issues. But now we need to review for just a moment.

Putting It on Paper

Last chapter we saw how important it is to ask the right kinds of questions. The best ones are simple, direct, "Should I" questions. Not surprisingly, they lend themselves perfectly to making a case for or against a decision.

In fact, the case is already implied. When you ask, "Should I?" there is already an unspoken "Should I not?" The pros and cons can easily be put on paper without evaluating them yet.

A Matter of Choice / 71

For example, suppose you were trying to decide whether to go to Big State Tech or to Small Local College. You could begin like this:

Decision Question: Should I go to Big State Tech?

Then by using brainstorming, you would begin to build the cases for and against going to Big State Tech. You would list all the reasons for going, and all the reasons against going.

After you were done your paper might look like this:

Decision Question: Should I go to Big State Tech?

Case for BST	Case against BST
1. Academic challenge	1. More expensive
2. Enjoy a bigger school	2. Far away from home
3. Meet more people	3. Might get homesick
4. Learn to live away from home	4. Would not get personalized instruction
5. Better educational opportunities	5. Friends going to Small Local College
6. Stimulating atmosphere	6. Crummy dorms
7. Diploma prestige	
8. New experience	
9. Better sports program	

That's all there is to it. Almost any "Should I" decision can be laid out the same way. This system is a balance sheet approach to evaluation because it weighs all the positives against all the negative considerations.

But you must be objective when using the balance sheet approach. Sometimes you will have an unconscious emotional bias toward one side or the

72 / Decisions! Decisions! Decisions!

other before you even set up the case. If you're not careful, your attitude will tilt the balance unfairly one way or the other. The secret is to be fair and honest in listing the reasons for and against, so the balance sheet will reflect the true situation. Otherwise you will just write down what you have already decided you would like to do.

Remember that evaluation comes later. You can't decide a thing at this point, or judge the merits of one case over the other. Your only concern in Step #2 is to examine the options. Gather the information and present the cases clearly and fairly, using brainstorming techniques to build your case.

The balance sheet approach can be set up in various ways, and it can be used for any number of alternatives that enter into a decision. Just make a separate balance sheet for each "Should I" question. The main idea is to get all the considerations (pro and con) on paper. Once you have done that, you're ready to move to Step #3, weighing the options.

But before you go get the bathroom scale, take a few minutes to review what you've learned in this chapter. Work through a decision question of your own. Begin with a "Should I" question, make a column for and against each case, and brainstorm each option. Learning how to weigh the options in chapter 7 will be much more rewarding if you think of a personal example to start with now.

7
LOOK BEFORE YOU LEAP

Suppose you wanted to buy a used car. You go to the used car lot, start looking around, and come across an old blue Dodge. A salesman strolls over and says, "Beauty, ain't she? Take her for a spin, and if you like her she's yours for $600" (which is about all you can afford).

You get in, turn the key, and the car starts all right. You drive around the block and it runs fine. The brakes, the horn, and the lights all work.

"How about it?" asks the salesman when you return. "You like it? It's yours."

Now it's time to make a decision. You quickly run through all the information at your disposal: the motor works, it has four wheels, it's the right price.

"OK," you say, "I'll take it." You've just bought yourself a used car. But was it the best one you could have bought?

How Low Can You Go?

We have been learning to make decisions on a rational basis. The process may be a foreign concept if you are used to going with your "gut feelings." Even though playing your hunches sometimes works, it usually fails.

Our feelings, by and large, are unstable indicators, liable to be up one moment and down the next. They cannot be depended on to consistently provide the best judgment. A decision made solely on the strength of an emotional surge is usually regretted later on.

One way to avoid making decisions we will later regret is to stay away from a process known as *minimizing*. I remember a kid in school who would raise his hand just as the instructor was passing out the test papers. He would ask, "What's the lowest grade I can get and still pass?" That's minimizing.

We do the same thing when we base our decisions on our feelings. We purposely don't invest much in a decision so we won't feel too bad if it doesn't work out. We look for the choice that seems to offer the least potential for disaster, while still satisfying the decision to be made. We settle for an option that is "good enough," rather than "best." We wrongly assume that if we don't set our goals too high, we won't fall as far when we miss.

Minimizing is wrong. It may allow you to get by for a while, but it eventually destroys the final goal of decision-making because it robs you of happiness. How can you be happy living at your minimum potential? You might be satisfied with an old blue Dodge that runs, but wouldn't you be happier with a newer car in better condition for the same price?

The Rush to Judgment

When your decision-making process rests solely on an emotional base, you quit weighing the evidence as soon as the most basic considerations are met. For example, suppose you have a cavity in your back molar. You might take a couple of aspirins to make the pain stop. The aspirins are a quick fix—a minimum effort to solve a major problem. When they wear off, you will still have your toothache. So you try a stronger painkiller, which also wears off after a while. Finally, you would go to the dentist and have him fix it. If he said the tooth had to come out, you would have him pull it. But if you hadn't minimized the problem to begin with, you could have gone directly to the dentist and saved a lot of time.

The challenge of decision-making creates a kind of psychological pain or stress which—like a toothache—must be dealt with immediately. In order to escape the pain, most people search for a quick fix—anything that will satisfy them easily and immediately.

Many people make poor decisions because they cannot resist making judgments on the first options they think of. Rather than taking time to brainstorm thoroughly, they *rush to judgment* on any alternative that comes to mind. It may or may not be the *best* course of action, but they are satisfied if it meets their minimum requirements.

When the evaluation process is cut short by minimizing, the result is often a weak solution that will be regretted later. The "quick fix" doesn't work in decision-making because we have to live with the results long after the choice has been made. It only makes sense to take time to carefully weigh *all* the options before thinking the plan through.

The Lawyer and the Judge

In Step #2 (examining the options), the idea was to play detective and search for the facts, gathering all available information for every alternative. And like a good legal advocate, you did not pass judgment on the alternatives. You just gathered information and built your case.

Now in Step #3 (weighing the options), you have the chance to play judge. You begin to examine all the facts, carefully consider the evidence, and make judgments on the cases presented to you.

While you (the lawyer) should be totally non-critical regarding options and alternatives, you (the judge) must be extremely critical and make discerning judgments. If, while weighing the options, you think of yourself as a sober-minded, eagle-eyed, objective judge, you'll be right on course in the decision-making process.

The lawyer makes a balance sheet to list facts for and against a certain option or alternative. He writes everything down on paper to see more objectively, and he is not as likely to forget an important point. The balance sheet created in Step #2 is also used in Step #3 by the judge to help weigh the various options.

Should all facts, options, alternatives, and choices receive the same consideration? Absolutely not. If all factors were equal, there would be no need to *weigh* the evidence. A judge must listen to the facts and decide what value to place on them. Some points will be of major importance, while others will be relatively unimportant. So you must look at your balance sheet and begin to assign values to each consideration you have listed.

(Of course, weighing the various alternatives only applies when there are no overriding spiritual principles involved. Why spend precious time and energy weighing evidence about whether to become an exotic dancer over Christmas vacation or to swipe the wheels off the neighbor's sports car? As we saw earlier, Christians already have a verdict for those kinds of decisions. "To one who knows the right thing to do, and does not do it, to him it is sin" [James 4:17, NASB].)

The Scale

To weigh anything you need a scale. A scale that weighs the importance of the various considerations in decision-making might look like this:

78 / Decisions! Decisions! Decisions!

1 = Minor Importance
2 = Significant
3 = Very Significant
4 = Important
5 = Extremely Important

Minor Importance—A consideration hardly worth mentioning. But since you bothered to write it down, it should receive a value.

Significant—A factor that matters to you, though not a great deal. Something to be recognized and considered.

Very Significant—A consideration that matters a great deal. Should not be overlooked in the final analysis.

Important—Something you feel strongly about. Has great impact on the decision.

Extremely Important—A consideration which is absolutely critical. Outweighs all others in seriousness.

Using the Scale

Now that we've assigned a weight to each degree of importance, let's see how the scale can be used on the balance sheet.

We'll continue the example we started in the last chapter of trying to decide whether to go to Big State Tech or to Small Local College.

Look Before You Leap / 79

The balance sheet looked like this:

Case for BST	Case against BST
1. Academic challenge	1. More expensive
2. Enjoy a bigger school	2. Far away from home
3. Meet more people	3. Might get homesick
4. Learn to live away from home	4. Would not get personalized instruction
5. Better educational opportunities	5. Friends going to Small Local College
6. Stimulating atmosphere	6. Crummy dorms
7. Diploma prestige	
8. New experience	
9. Better sports program	

Now, using the scale, here's how one person might weigh the consideration *for* BST:

Case for BST

1. Academic challenge	2
2. Enjoy a bigger school	1
3. Meet more people	1
4. Learn to live away from home	3
5. Better educational opportunities	4
6. Stimulating atmosphere	3
7. Diploma prestige	1
8. New experience	2
9. Better sports program	1
TOTAL	18

Analysis—In the case for Big State Tech, the person felt that the academic challenge of a larger school was more significant than its size or sports program. Learning to live away from home was a definite consideration as was the value of a more stimulating atmosphere. But he rated the greatest importance as the better educational opportunities that the larger school offered.

Now let's see how he weighed the considerations *against* going to Big State Tech.

Case against BST
1. More expensive — 5
2. Far away from home — 3
3. Might get homesick — 3
4. Would not get personalized instruction — 1
5. Friends going to Small Local College — 4
6. Crummy dorms — 2
TOTAL — 18

Analysis—Money was the most important consideration by far in this case, since going to the bigger school would take more money for living expenses and tuition. Another result might be the need to get a job, which would take away from studies and free time. The school was also farther away, which would mean fewer trips home and increase the likelihood of homesickness. The next highest importance was placed on continuing friendships with people going to Small Local College. Housing and nonpersonalized instruction were seen as problems, but not exceptional ones.

Of course, you would have filled out the balance sheet differently, weighing some considerations higher and others lower. This scale is subjective, and the assignment of any value is up to you. No two people would weigh their feelings exactly alike.

Look Before You Leap / 81

If you fudge here and there because of an emotional bias toward one case or the other, you weaken the whole process. Always be as honest as you can.

Scoring

Notice that both cases we judged came out with a total of 18 points. Does that mean that both cases are exactly equal? That either alternative would be the same?

No, because the cases had a different number of considerations. The total scores must be divided by the number of elements in each case to arrive at a final score. Only then can we balance the scale. The following equation will be helpful:

$T \div C = FS$

The *total* (the sum of the points of all considerations) divided by the number of *considerations* equals the *final score*.

The case *for* BST had a *total* of 18 points and 9 *considerations*, so the *final score* is 2 (18 ÷ 9). The case *against* BST also had 18 points, but only 6 considerations, so the final score is 3 (18 ÷ 6). But what do these final scores mean?

Simply put, the final score represents the *average* point value assigned to each case. The final score for the case *for* BST was 2, and the final score for the case *against* BST was 3. Turning back to our scale of importance, we can see that the difference between 2 and 3 is a difference between "Significant" and "Very Significant." So the case *against*

82 / Decisions! Decisions! Decisions!

BST has the advantage. Its considerations, though fewer, outweigh those of the other case. Of the two alternatives, the weighed evidence points toward going to Small Local College.

"Terrific!" you say. "Now can I make a final decision?"

Not necessarily. What you have done is merely clarified the alternatives and given weight to all the considerations—a process that sorts out all the information. But if you find yourself unhappy or uneasy with your result, perhaps you haven't been exactly honest with yourself in the scoring process. Or maybe there are other considerations you haven't listed on the balance sheet.

If so, go back and try it again. Include the new considerations and try to be more honest with yourself and your feelings. See what happens.

Decision Indicators

The final score is *not* the decision. It is what we might call a "decision indicator." The point score only suggests the direction the decision might take based on the evidence you have presented. If the final scores are close, you still can't be too sure of what decision to make. But the greater the distance between the final scores of each case, the greater confidence you can have in making a decision.

If, for example, the final score in the case *for* BST was 2, and the final score *against* BST was 4, you would have a *very* strong indication for choosing not to attend the large school. But what if you don't like that result? What if, even after weighing all the evidence, you still *want* to go to BST?

Clearly, you must have very good reasons for going against the weight of your own evidence. And if you do, those reasons should be listed as considerations on the balance sheet. But if you can't come up with any additional reasons and you're sure you've been honest with yourself, it is likely that you are reacting emotionally to the decision indicated by the final score.

To deny evidence because of emotions is dangerous. Whenever you make a decision against your better judgment, you set yourself up for a big letdown later on. Perhaps you could sleep on it and try the balance sheet later, when you have time to reconsider the situation.

If you are in basic agreement with the direction shown by the decision indicators, and if you have been honest throughout all the steps of the decision process, you might be ready to make a decision.

The balance sheet process can be used to try any number of alternatives against others. Compare two options, weigh the "winner" against another alternative, and continue the process until you have tried all your options. The one that is left is the strongest indicator for the decision at hand.

Weighing Spiritual Considerations

At this point in the decision-making process, we

84 / Decisions! Decisions! Decisions!

must examine the alternative that comes out on top and see if any spiritual considerations apply. We have said that Christians often must examine certain spiritual considerations in their decisions. Factors which are based on biblical principles or moral ethics might have an influence on the issue to be decided.

Whenever spiritual considerations do apply to a decision, they should always be given higher values than the other considerations. Why? The reason is simple: as Christians, our first priority is to live as Christ would like us to.

Spiritual considerations are very tricky, and not at all easy to fit into a formula. But the best general rule is that they take precedence over other considerations.

"What?" you say. "You mean after all this examining and weighing, you just toss the balance sheet aside?"

Yes. *All the cold logic of the decision-making method can be overridden by a simple spiritual principle.* And Christians need to take a close look at their decisions to make sure they consider the spiritual aspect of each one.

Using our example of Big State Tech vs. Small Local College, let's introduce a spiritual consideration and see what difference it might make. Remember, the evidence presented so far weighed in favor of going to Small Local College. But suppose we find out that SLC is an elite private school that does not allow blacks or Latinos as students. Maybe you're not black or Latino and could still be admitted. How do you weigh this consideration?

Individual conscience plays an important part. If you don't view racial discrimination as a spiritual issue, you would give the consideration the appropriate 1 to 5 rating, figure up the final score, and see what happens.

But some people consider racial discrimination a moral, ethical, and spiritual issue they cannot and will not ignore. They feel that the school's policy contradicts biblical teaching: "There is neither Jew nor Greek, slave nor free, male nor female, for you are all one in Christ Jesus (Galatians 3:28). For those people, this one spiritual principle outweighs all other possible considerations. Therefore, as far as they are concerned, attending SLC is out of the question.

Spiritual considerations often bring to light such gray areas. So as soon as a spiritual consideration enters your decision-making process, you must go to God in prayer and ask for His wisdom and guidance.

We sometimes lose sight of the underlying spiritual principles behind much of what we do. We need to spend time reading the Bible, praying, and nurturing our faith. We need to improve our spiritual eyesight to better discern when spiritual details are involved in the decisions we face, so we can see them more clearly. Only then can we make decisions that we (and God) can be proud of.

8
WAITING AND DEBATING

Everyone who knew Eddie also knew that he was a show-off—especially when there were girls around. One December evening Eddie and two of his friends were walking through the park with their ice skates, heading for the neighborhood pond. When they arrived they found a group of girls had also shown up, but no one was skating.

"The sign says *THIN ICE*," one of the girls said.

"That doesn't mean anything," said Eddie, quickly putting on his skates. "Watch this!"

They all watched as Eddie speedskated out onto the center of the pond and speedsank into the water as the ice gave way. The fire department had to come fish Eddie out of the pond, and he ended up spending Christmas in the hospital with double pneumonia and frostbite.

Eddie's problem—aside from being a jerk—was that he never stopped to think about the possible results of his decision. He never stopped to ask himself, *What will happen if I do this?* or even, *Can I handle the consequences?* Eddie's unquestioned commitment to his decision proved disastrous.

We must live with the results of every decision we make. The bigger the decision, the more we have riding on the outcome—and the greater our reluctance to take the final plunge. Anytime we make a decision without considering the consequences, we are "skating on thin ice."

Even minor decisions like what color socks to put on in the morning can give us grief. If any of you guys have ever worn white socks with a dress suit, you know how painful it can be when even small decisions backfire.

But we can prevent many of the disastrous results that come from hasty decisions. Of the five steps of decision-making we have mentioned so far, this fourth one is probably the easiest to recognize. Step #4 is *thinking the plan through*, the "Should I" step.

In the decision-making process you have already sized up the situation, examined the options, and weighed the options. You have a strong indication of what you ought to do. Now it's time to sit back and ask yourself, "Should I really do it?"

The Great Debate

Asking that question as you stand at the brink of a momentous decision will often set off a great internal debate. You begin to bounce questions off the walls of your brain as you try to imagine how the decision will affect you.

Suppose you are toying with the idea of running for class president. You have just about made up your mind to announce your candidacy, but not quite. Most likely you'd find yourself in a heated internal debate over the outcome of the decision. Your mental argument might go something like this:

You'll look like a jerk up there on the platform with all the other candidates.

No, I won't. I'll look just fine.

Everyone will laugh at you.

They laugh at all *the candidates.*

Is politics really something you want to get involved in?

Sure, it will be a good experience for me.

Except that no one will vote for you.

Lots of people will vote for me. Even if I don't win, I'll make lots of new friends.

There are easier ways to make friends. Besides, running for class president won't do much for your grades.

My grades are all right. Besides, if I were class president I could see about getting the dress code eased up a little. That would make a lot of people very happy.

There's more to life than happiness, you know.

Right. There's risking myself, trying new things, and maybe growing in the process. Running for class president would be the right thing for me to do.

As you begin to think the plan through, you look at the decision, try it on for size, examine it from different angles, back up and put it in proper perspective, and try to mentally role play the situation as if you had already made the decision. You stand back to picture the effect your intended course of action will have on your life. This thinking process is your last chance to try out the decision before plunging ahead.

Some people get this far in decision-making and then freeze up. Others just jump over this essential step and dive into the decision with no thought at all. The problem in both extremes is that the person just can't stand the suspense.

BST vs. SLC . . . the Envelope, Please

Let's go back to our example of choosing a college and think that plan through. After weighing the various considerations for and against Big State Tech, the balance sheet looked like this:

Case for BST
1. Academic challenge	2
2. Enjoy a bigger school	1
3. Meet more people	1
4. Learn to live away from home	3
5. Better educational opportunities	4
6. Stimulating atmosphere	3
7. Diploma prestige	1
8. New experience	2
9. Better sports program	1
TOTAL	18

Total (18) ÷ *Considerations* (9) = Final Score (2)

Case against BST
1. More expensive   5
2. Far away from home   3
3. Might get homesick   3
4. Would not get personalized
   instruction   1
5. Friends going to local college   4
6. Crummy dorms   2
   TOTAL   18

Total (18) ÷ *Considerations* (6) = *Final Score* (3)

We said that a comparison of the final scores gave a slight indication in favor of going to Small Local College. In this particular decision there were no overriding spiritual considerations, so we are free to think about what a decision to go to Small Local College might mean.

Here's where you need to think the plan through and ask those mental questions, such as:

Is SLC right for me?

What will people think of me for going to a small college?

Can I handle the results of this decision?

Notice that these are not the same kinds of questions asked before. They deal not with considerations *for* or *against* making the decision, but rather with the *impact* of the decision. When thinking the plan through it is important to examine the possible emotional or psychological effects of the decision.

So far we have only stressed the rational approach to decision-making. Emotions confuse the

Waiting and Debating / 91

process during the first three steps. But now we are going to put feelings in their proper place. They belong here—in Step #4.

After all of the factual data has been gathered, sifted, and evaluated to reach the most logical solution, then you are free to let your emotions try out the proposed decision. You let your inner self take the decision out for a spin to see how it feels on the road.

If you feel good about the proposed decision after your emotional test drive, you are ready to go on to the next step. If you don't feel good about the decision, you might have more work to do.

Like we said before, just because you feel good about a decision doesn't mean it is right. And feeling bad about a decision doesn't necessarily mean it is wrong, either. Often an uncomfortable feeling only means that you're having trouble seeing yourself going through with the decision you are considering.

For example, you might actually wish you were going to Big State Tech. In your mind's eye you can see all the great football games and campus activities. But all the facts indicate that Small Local College would be the better decision. Your emotions have a hard time adjusting to what your brain has worked through.

That's OK. Part of thinking the plan through involves taking a short "time-out" to prepare yourself for the outcome before going through with the decision. You want to discover whether you *can* commit yourself to the course of action you have chosen.

Prayer and Waiting

Thinking the plan through is an especially critical step for Christians. They have an additional resource they can call into play—prayer. The time to pray is not *after* you've already made up your mind, and not *before* you've defined the decision for yourself. The time to pray is when God's help and guidance will actually have a bearing on your decision.

We are often guilty of asking God's blessing on our already-made decisions, rather than including Him in the process. God can guide us through *all* the steps of decision-making, but His presence is most keenly needed in this stage of thinking the plan through.

The Bible details the crucial importance of prayer at this point. Everyone is familiar with the story of Jesus in the Garden of Gethsemane (Matthew 26:36-46). It is one of the most poignant passages in the Bible.

After what would be His last supper, Jesus took His disciples to a place called Gethsemane. He went there to pray, knowing that He was in His final hours on earth. In terrible anguish He cried out, "My Father, if it is possible, may this cup be taken from Me. Yet not as I will, but as You will" (v. 39). He prayed so fervently and was so troubled that His sweat was like great drops of blood (Luke 22:44).

What was the purpose of Jesus' prayer? Was He trying to get out of God's plan for Him? Was He attempting to bargain with God?

Not at all. In classic style, Jesus was thinking through the plan for the decision He was about to make. His prayer was for strength to carry out the decision He saw before Him. He was surrendering Himself to God's will.

As followers of Christ we can draw on that same source of strength and wisdom for our decisions. In Step #4 we can use prayer to help us center our hearts in God's will, and to focus our minds on the decision at hand.

Waiting is also important. In thinking the plan through, it is never a bad idea to simply step back and wait. Put the decision on hold while you pray about it. This is not at all the same thing as putting off the decision. It is simply providing time to allow God to guide you, speak to you, and move you closer to His will.

Waiting gives you an opportunity to view the decision in perspective. It gives your emotions a chance to adjust. Many times bad decisions are made, not because they are wrong, but because they are rushed. This is especially true with decisions of a highly emotional nature—such as whether or not to get married. Generally speaking, the higher the emotional impact of the decision, the more time you should allow yourself to think about it.

How Much Is Enough?

How much prayerful waiting is enough? No standard guidelines exist—a few minutes, a couple of hours, a few days, or a week or more. It all depends on the decision, your preparation for the decision, and God's timing. "The Lord is good to those whose hope is in Him, to the one who seeks Him; it is good to wait quietly for the salvation of the Lord" (Lamentations 3:25-26).

It might help to ask yourself a few questions at the beginning of the deliberation period, and not continue until you can answer them. What kinds of questions? The same kinds of questions we talked about before, except with a more direct Christian emphasis. For instance:

Will my decision hurt anyone?
Will it make me a better person?
Will the result be spiritually helpful or harmful?
Will it cause anyone else to stumble in his Christian growth?
Would God approve of my decision?
Will it bring glory to God?

When you can answer these questions to your satisfaction, then your plan has been well thought through. If you have trouble with one or more of them, you may need to spend additional time seeking God's guidance. Or maybe it's time to go back to an earlier step and examine other options.

You Can't Fleece God

Some Christians use a practice called "putting out the fleece" to help them make tough decisions. The name comes from a story in the Old Testament about a young man named Gideon. He was chosen

Waiting and Debating / 95

by God to lead an army to save Israel from her enemies (Judges 6—8).

Now Gideon, understandably, was having a little trouble accepting his role as leader of the army. He decided to put God to the test to see if he had indeed understood the situation correctly. He told God, "If You *are* going to save Israel by my hand, as You have said, I need to be sure. I'll put a sheepskin out on the ground tonight. In the morning, if it's wet with dew, I'll know You're serious about this" (Judges 6:36-37, author's paraphrase).

The next morning the fleece was wet with dew and the ground all around it was dry. But Gideon still had doubts. He said to God, "Please don't get mad at me, but let me try just one more test. This time let the sheepskin be dry while all the ground around it is wet with dew. Then I'll know that You mean business" (Judges 6:39, author's paraphrase).

God also went along with this second request. The next morning Gideon found the fleece dry and all the ground around it wet with dew. It is to Gideon's credit that he didn't persist any longer with his fleece technique. He finally did what God had asked.

Many Christians believe that if they are undecided or uncertain about something, they can "put out a fleece," figuratively speaking, and God will show them what to do. A modern example might be something like:

God, if You want me to take Algebra II during second period, let the class be open. If not, let it be closed. Or: *God, if I'm supposed to go out for wrestling, let the coach call me tonight. If not, don't have him call.*

The idea, of course, is to get God to send a special sign your way to point out in no uncertain terms what you should do and how you should do it. The only trouble with that system is that God doesn't work that way.

While He may have allowed Gideon, in an age of doubt and uncertainty, to put Him to the test, He has made it clear that we are to live before Him in *faith*. "Do not put the Lord your God to the test" (Luke 4:12).

"Putting out the fleece" seeks to sidestep faith altogether by forcing God to send personal messages. But, if God granted personal interviews to all Christians, there would be no need for faith at all.

"We live by faith, not by sight," the Apostle Paul explains (2 Corinthians 5:7). By faith, we expect God to take part in our decision-making process.

Waiting and debating are essential elements in that process, but they can't go on forever. We must learn to take action (also by faith) and move ahead. *How* we do that is the subject of the next chapter.

9
THE MIND OF CHRIST

What do the following people have in common?
- an alligator wrestler
- a guy who dresses "punk" for his sister's wedding
- a person who shouts "Movie!" in a crowded firehouse
- a stunt man

Give up? Each one is a person for whom the initials O.O.H.M. have a special meaning. The letters stand for "Out Of His Mind," a phrase that applies to everyone listed above.

Actually, you don't have to be absolutely, incurably crazy to be out of your mind. In fact, the phrase doesn't even imply insanity at all—just quirky, odd, or unusual behavior. "Out of his mind" is one of several terms to describe a person's mental state.

For example, you can speak your mind, give

98 / Decisions! Decisions! Decisions!

someone a piece of your mind, bear something in mind, make up your mind, or put your mind at ease. When two people find themselves in complete agreement about something, they are said to be of like minds.

The Apostle Paul tells Christians that, "we have the mind of Christ" (1 Corinthians 2:16). What exactly does he mean?

In Your Right Mind

The mind, most people would recognize, is not just the brain. The brain is the organ that makes thinking possible. But the mind is more than *thinking*; it is *thought* itself. More precisely, it is *you* as expressed in your thoughts.

If your mind is the real *you*, then the mind of Christ is really *Christ*. It is that part of Christ which can be expressed in thought.

When a person becomes a Christian, Christ lives in him. The part of the person that saw life a certain way, behaved a certain way, and thought a certain way, is transformed. He isn't the same person anymore. Paul writes, "If anyone is in Christ, he is a new creation; the old has gone, the new has come!"(2 Corinthians 5:17)

For a Christian to have the mind of Christ means that he has the ability to understand life as Christ Himself sees it. Through faith, Christ's thoughts can become his thoughts. You might even say that someone goes from being "out of his mind" as a non-Christian, to being "in his right mind" as a

Christian, consciously trying to submit every thought to God's will.

Having the mind of Christ involves more than just the so-called spiritual side of life: Bible reading, prayer, worship, and Christian fellowship. It can involve every aspect of life—if we let it.

Heads and Hearts

It's easy to believe that we are being spiritual when we *feel* spiritual. The rest of the time we just go along as our normal, everyday, ordinary selves. But the truth is that when we become Christians, all of life becomes spiritual.

This is sometimes hard to understand because so often we equate "spiritual" with "emotional." We think something is spiritual because we get a warm feeling from it. No doubt this stems from the obvious fact that many times spiritual experiences *are* emotional experiences. So we get the idea that we're most spiritual when we're most emotional.

But true spirituality involves the head just as much as the heart. This is perhaps the very point Paul was trying to make when he spoke about having the mind of Christ. In this book we have been talking about developing a *rational* method of making decisions as opposed to an *emotional* approach. But being rational does not mean being unspiritual.

Saying things like, "I'll just trust the Lord to show me what to do," or, "I'll have faith God will lead me where I should go," does not make you more spiritual in your approach to making decisions. You are not more spiritual because you blindly cast your unthinking self into life.

You can use your God-given mental faculties to size up the situation, examine and weigh options, think the plan through, and put a decision into effect. Yet all this can be done with the secure knowledge that the part of your mind that works through the process is the mind of Christ working within you.

Lack of Sense

In the movie, *The Emigrants*, a boat full of devout country folk came to America to escape political and religious persecution and famine in their homeland. While on their way across the ocean many of the emigrants met together to study English, their new language. But one young woman steadfastly refused to take part in the English classes. When asked why, the young lady replied, "What is the use? God knows where He is sending me. When I arrive I will know how to speak English."

Many of us fall into similar traps when it comes to decision-making. Like the girl who believed she would suddenly be able to speak English the moment she set foot on American soil, we sometimes act as if the decision will miraculously materialize when we need it—all without a moment's preparation. What we believe to be a powerful faith is actually a powerful lack of sense.

God does move in people's hearts, but He also moves in their minds. He is in the warm, spontaneous outpourings of love and joy from the heart, and He is also in the logical, reasoned thinking of the mind.

Becoming Like Christ

You may be thinking, *It's OK to talk about having the mind of Christ, but I know some of my thoughts are not the least bit Christlike.* That condition is true of all of us. But just because we have lapses, or periods when we are out of touch with Christ doesn't mean that Christ has deserted us. It only means that we are not living up to our full potential as Christians.

Becoming like Christ would not be possible if we did not already have the mind of Christ to guide us and help us. Spiritual growth is still a struggle—a process full of straining, striving, and making mistakes. No one starts his Christian life being exactly like Christ. But we set Christlikeness as a goal and grow toward it. We have the mind of Christ to help us become more like Him.

Paul compares this growth process to a race that you run, trying to win the prize (1 Corinthians 9:24). But to run this race and win it, you must know Christ. You must get to know Him as well as you know your best friend.

And you come to know Christ as you would anyone else—through a close personal relationship. By regularly spending time together, sharing yourself with Him, and putting your faith and trust in Him, you gradually become more like Him. When you know a friend as well as you know yourself, you can tell how he would react when a decision needs to be made. As you develop the mind of Christ, you will have His guidance as you face tough decisions.

This is our goal as Christian decision-makers—to have such a close relationship with Christ, to know Him so well, that our thoughts are His thoughts and His thoughts are our very own.

10
TIME TO ACT

We have at long last come to the fifth and final step of our decision-making process: putting the decision into effect.

"Wait just a minute," you say. "I haven't even reached a decision yet."

Quite right. No decision is ever "reached" until it is put into action. Up to this point you have been poking, probing, and pushing around all kinds of ideas—important parts of the process—but now it's time for you to take your best shot and put your decision into operation.

Before you do, let's step back a moment and recap the procedure to this point.

Step #1—*Sizing up the situation*. You became aware of a challenge to your normal way of life. You gauged the nature of the challenge to determine if action was necessary. You became satisfied that the situation warranted some kind of action.

Step #2—*Examining the options.* You began to assemble information which would help you determine what form the required action should take. You accumulated and became familiar with the choices for action that were open to you.

Step #3—*Weighing the options.* You examined all your possible options and evaluated them carefully to determine which one offered the best result.

Step #4—*Thinking the plan through.* You selected the best option and began to consider it as the final solution to the problem posed by the challenge. You "tried on" that option and imagined the possible outcome if it were put into effect. You looked for assurance that the proposed decision was right for you.

Step #5—*Putting the decision into effect.* Now you need to take the necessary steps to put your decision into operation.

The Big Freeze-up

What could be simpler? Once you have thundered through brainstorming sessions, balanced balance sheets, worn out your calculator getting scores for all the different cases, it seems that putting the decision into action would be the simplest step of all. All you have to do is *do it!*

But sometimes this last step is the hardest. You stand on the brink, ready to make the leap into the vast unknown, and suddenly freeze. In spite of the fact that you have sized up, examined, weighed, and thought the plan through so you know what

Time to Act / 105

your decision should be, you stop short of taking action. You choke. The decision-making process grinds to a screeching halt.

What happened? It's that ever-threatening enemy—fear—back again to botch up everything you've done.

As the time for taking action draws closer, you begin to experience doubts as anxiety raises its oily head. You hear a worried voice whispering in your ear, *What if you blow it? What if you don't do the right thing? You could ruin everything!*

This sudden lack of confidence is quite normal. It arises from your awareness of the importance of the decision. Obviously, you move through the day making decisions without becoming paralyzed with fear. You don't spend hours agonizing over what kind of cereal to have for breakfast. You don't stand in silent indecision when it comes time to decide whether to put on a jacket or a sweater.

It's fair to say that as the risks increase, so does the fear. If the stakes are high, you'll probably feel at least a little frightened about taking that final step to put the decision into motion.

When faced with tough, life-shaping decisions, it is normal to feel a little squeamish. After all, choosing the wrong college, the wrong career, or the wrong marriage partner is no small mistake.

At this point I could come on with a knowing, fatherly attitude and say something like, "Relax. There's nothing to be afraid of. It's all in your head."

Such a comment might sound good, but it would certainly be misleading. The truth is that

106 / Decisions! Decisions! Decisions!

fear is there. It grows out of your concern for your life, your happiness, and the happiness of those around you. The presence of fear is a normal and healthy sign that you understand the importance of the situation.

The decision, however, must be made. You can't stand forever on the brink, too fearful to take the leap. And you shouldn't give up your independence and let someone else make the decision for you. It comes down to you.

What should you do?

You do the mature, responsible thing. You act. You don't disregard your fear, downplay it, or rationalize it away. You act in spite of it.

Look at all you have put into the decision so far—all the hard work you have done. If you have laid the proper foundation, carefully gone through every step, and tried to be as honest as possible, then you've done all you can do. So now you can go ahead and take action in spite of how you feel about the decision. You let your head take the wheel and put your fear in the backseat.

Fear itself isn't wrong and isn't anything to be ashamed of. But it must not be allowed to undo all the work you have done. Don't let your fear paralyze you or talk you into allowing someone else to make your decision.

Walking on Water

The New Testament records a relevant story that shows the negative impact fear can make on a

Time to Act / 107

good decision. The account is found in Matthew 14:22-36.

Jesus had just finished feeding 5,000 people who had gathered to hear Him. He sent His disciples ahead of Him in a boat while He dismissed the crowds and then went up in the hills alone to pray.

Evening came, the boat drifted out from the shore, and the wind rose against it. Jesus went to join His disciples in the middle of the night, walking on the water. Naturally, the disciples had never seen anything like it. They became afraid. Someone said, "It's a ghost!"

But ever-practical Peter called out, "Lord, if it's You, tell me to come to You on the water."

Jesus said, "Come."

Peter got out of the boat and started walking on the water toward Jesus. He had just about reached Him when he looked around, felt the wind on his face, saw the waves surging around him, and became afraid. Instantly he started sinking. "Lord, save me!" he cried.

Jesus reached out His hand and caught him. "You of little faith," He said, "why did you doubt?"

Doubt and fear are enemies of faith. They will destroy it if we allow them to. Peter's faith allowed him to walk on water, and he was doing fine until his fear surfaced. His fear made him doubt, his doubt overpowered his faith, and as a result he nearly drowned.

Making a tough decision is a little like walking on water. There comes a time when you have to leave the boat and step out on the waves. It's normal to wonder what is going to hold you up. It's normal to fear the rolling water around you. But the secret is to keep your doubts and fears down to a normal, manageable size. You cannot let your insecurity get so big that it blots out your faith.

At this point we should clarify the *object* of our faith in the decision-making process. Our faith is not in the *process* we use to make our decisions. It is not in *our own ability* to make decisions. Nor is it in the *decision itself*.

Our faith is in Jesus—the only proper object of faith for all decision-makers and water-walkers. We trust in Christ and we have faith that He will walk with us through the shifting seas of our lives.

As we peer from the side of the boat, Jesus says, "Come." Faith means getting up, confidently taking that first step out of the boat, and walking on the water with eyes fixed on Christ, who walks with us.

Water-walking faith takes commitment—not only to Christ, but also to the decision we have reached. It is not possible to walk with one foot on the water and one in the boat. Having arrived at a logical decision, you must commit yourself to it, pursue it, and put it into action.

Until you take action, the decision isn't official. Only when you have started the machinery of your decision in motion—when you have acted on it—is it a decision at all. The Bible says that faith without works is dead (James 2:17, 26). So is a decision without action. Without action the decision is never born.

Your Will, or God's?

Sometimes people hesitate when it comes time to take action because they don't know if the decision they have come to is God's will for them. They have prayed and waited on God, but haven't received any special leading one way or the other about what they should do. They ask for a sign, and the signs are unclear and inconclusive. Then they don't know *what* to do.

Such was the case with Harold. He was a new Christian, and very concerned about remaining in God's will at all times. One day he was offered the opportunity to go with some people his age on a week-long retreat. They were to help develop the leadership skills of newer Christians thinking about going to college.

Harold thought the retreat would be good, and he wanted to go. But it would conflict with the Bible study and prayer group he had committed himself to attending. He didn't know what to do.

Should he go on the retreat, and miss several group meetings? Or should he stay home and attend the group sessions, but miss the chance to learn some valuable new skills? He couldn't decide, so he prayed about it and waited. Then he prayed again and waited some more.

The deadline for signing up for the retreat was fast approaching and he still had not received a clear idea of what to do. Certainly God wanted him to become a better leader among his peers. But God also wanted him to be faithful to the commitment he had made to his prayer group.

110 / Decisions! Decisions! Decisions!

Exactly what *was* God's will for him in this situation?

If you have ever been in a situation similar to Harold's, you know how frustrating it can be. You want God to show you what to do. Nothing major—just a nod or a wink to let you know how to proceed. But God is silent.

Unfortunately, there is no general rule of thumb for situations like this. It would be a big help to us if we could point to Rule #62 in the *Christian Rulebook:*

"Oh, yes. It says here that when you have two conflicting choices you should always select the one offering the greatest opportunity for spiritual growth. However, in cases where prior commitments exist, they supersede any other choice(s)."

"Supersede? What's that mean?"

"It means you can't go on the retreat. You have to stay home and meet with the prayer group. You have a prior commitment."

A rule book would be handy, no doubt, but we don't have anything like that. In spite of the help we can get from Scripture, prayer, and the support of other Christians, it seems as if God—in some situations—is determined to make us choose for ourselves. He refuses to send down His answer, forcing us to muddle through as best we can with no clear leading. Why?

Can it be that somehow in the agony of trying to find His will, to hear His call and follow Him, we experience spiritual growth? Perhaps in the struggle to resolve the issues that face us, we are stretching muscles that are not used nearly enough. Perhaps when we must grapple hand to hand with hard decisions we develop strength in areas where we need building up.

When God is silent, it is not because He doesn't care what we do. But perhaps God doesn't care as much whether Harold goes on a retreat or stays home as He does that Harold learns to make those kinds of decisions on his own.

It seems that sometimes we get so caught up with the question, "Am I doing this by my will, or God's will?" that we miss a fairly obvious answer. We search so hard for God's will for some specific situation that we miss what might be called God's "ultimate will." Above all else, God wants us to grow in grace and faith and wisdom and love, becoming closer to Him and to our fellowman.

When your decisions agree with God's ultimate will, you can be sure that what you desire for yourself is what God wants for you as well. Then you can walk in confidence, eyes fixed on Jesus, taking bold steps right above the waters of uncertainty. That's what I call putting a decision into effect.

11
IMPROVING YOUR FORESIGHT

Janet decided, after long and careful deliberation, to go to nursing school in a neighboring state. She enrolled and did her very best to keep up, but soon found she was just not as prepared as most of the other students. She began to feel that she had made the wrong decision to enter nursing.

Mike saved his money all summer so he could buy a used car. He decided to buy the car so he could get to work and school without having someone else driving him all the time. A few weeks after he bought the car, he discovered that it was a lemon that needed constant repair and upkeep.

Jean wanted an apartment of her own. She came from a large family and felt that her room at home could be well used by her younger sisters. She had a good job and was anxious to start paying her own way in the world. She discussed it with her parents who agreed that she should give it a try. She found an apartment and a roommate to share expenses and signed a one-year lease. After four months, though, her roommate was not able to pay her half of the rent and phone bills, and made plans to move out. Jean was stuck with twice her normal expenses, no roommate, and became sorry she'd ever left home in the first place.

20-20 Hindsight

It's often said that while people's foresight might be lousy, everyone has perfect 20-20 hindsight. That's true. You do tend to see a situation better *after* the fact. Long after it's too late to decide again, you know perfectly well what you *should* have done. That's hindsight for you.

"A lot of good it does," you say. Well, it might not be the best method of learning, but hindsight *can* be turned to good use if you know how.

You can use your perfect hindsight to evaluate decisions after you've made them. Then use what you learn from your evaluation to help you make better decisions in the future—to improve your foresight, in other words.

A lot of people say, "What good is evaluating a decision? After all if it's good, great! If it's bad, tough. Better luck next time."

After all, the hard labor it takes to make a decision and act on it, most of us would like to end the process there. Good decision-makers, however, always go through an evaluation period to see how the decision they have made is working out.

Evaluation is a necessary "sixth step" that does not come naturally, the way the other five do. The first five steps mirror what normally takes place in the brain to bring about action. You size up the situation, examine the options, weigh them, think the plan through, and put the decision into effect. The process is logical so far.

Evaluating the results of your decision is not as natural, but still just as necessary. The reluctance to evaluate is understandable. After investing a great amount of time and energy into making a major life decision, you just don't feel like going through it all over again. Besides, if you believe that God was leading you to make the decision you made, and to act as you did, it seems like a lack of faith to question the results. And if the decision is working out great, there's no need to evaluate it. Right?

Wrong. Human beings are peculiarly constructed. Even though we have eyes that look ahead, we cannot see very far into the future. We simply cannot know everything about a decision until after it has been made. And even though we try to anticipate every possibility and examine our decision from every angle, there is still a vast unknown territory we cannot foresee.

Like the moon, every decision has a side we never get to examine until after we get there. "Ah! But then it's too late!" you say. But you're not necessarily right.

Exploring the Great Unknown

The three examples at the beginning of this chapter had a common thread that ran through them. In each case, the decision turned out wrong from the decision-maker's point of view because each had an unknown quantity that made the decision backfire.

Janet had no way of knowing that she would not be as well prepared as the other students. How could she know that her high school education had let her down, and that she might need a year or two of junior college to catch up with the other students? How could Mike know that the car he had dreamed about and so carefully chosen would turn out to be a lemon? And how was Jean supposed to know that her roomie would turn out to be a deadbeat? How could she possibly foresee how miserable she would feel, and how many problems her decision would cause?

Short of a magical ability to foretell the future, Janet, Mike, and Jean—or anyone else, for that matter—have no way of knowing the outcome of their decisions. We don't see clearly through the glass of the future (1 Corinthians 13:12).

Whose Fault Is It?

So the next question is, "Whose fault is it?" Is it our fault our decisions sometimes go wrong because we can't foresee all the potential problems? Or is it really God's fault? After all, *He's* the one in

116 / Decisions! Decisions! Decisions!

charge of the future. And if we're diligently trying to follow Him, trying to do His will, why does He allow us to make bad decisions at all?

There are no easy answers. The truth is, nobody really knows for sure. But that doesn't keep a lot of people from attempting to answer in various ways.

They might say, "It's your fault because you didn't hear God correctly, so you were out of His will." Or they say, "It's no one's fault—God is just testing you." Or, "God's will is perfect. You didn't make a mistake. You just can't see His overall plan yet."

The only problem with these answers is that they don't really answer anything. The truth is that even when we do our decision-making homework properly, pray for guidance, wait for God's leading, and follow in faith, good decisions can still go bad.

People down through the ages have struggled with the same problem. In the Old and New Testaments we hear God's own people asking in chorus, over and over again, "Why, why, why?" "Why this way, God? Why not the other? I trusted You. Why did You let this happen? Why? Why? Why?"

And "Why?" is the one question God seldom answers. Perhaps He leaves it unanswered because it is the very heartbeat of our faith. Where is faith when we know all the answers? Why use a guide when you already know the way?

Could it be that our desire to know why, forever burning in our hearts and minds, actually keeps faith's embers glowing? Perhaps. But you can wonder endlessly, and it still doesn't help much when you're stuck with a bad situation because a decision blew up in your face.

Like everybody else, I've wondered about it, thought about it, and prayed about it. And I've never found a better explanation than this:

It is easier to steer a moving ship than one that's moored to the dock.

That old saying was applied to Christianity by David Howard and restated in a small pamphlet by Paul Little called, *Affirming the Will of God* (InterVarsity Press, p. 19). The pamphlet was helpful to me in many ways, but I've never forgotten that one idea. It sums up our situation when it comes to making a hard decision in the face of the vast unknown. We plan, we pray, we act, we go. We become a moving ship that God can steer however He wills.

We obviously cannot be steered in *any* direction, much less the right one, if we stay tied to the dock of indecision, waiting for the wind of God's will to fill our sails. So we move out in faith, making our plans and acting on them. Yet we still watch for God's signposts along the way. We may need to live through a few failed decisions to recognize God's great support of other decisions we have made. We may have to travel a road with a few rocky stretches so we will be grateful for the smooth places.

However you explain decisions that fall through, you can begin to understand what God told the Prophet Isaiah: "My thoughts are not your thoughts, neither are your ways My ways. . . . As

118 / Decisions! Decisions! Decisions!

the heavens are higher than the earth, so are My ways higher than your ways and My thoughts than your thoughts" (Isaiah 55:8-9).

Moving On

So what does all this discussion have to do with being stuck with a bad decision? Or with evaluating decisions, for that matter?

Only this: *Decisions are not set in concrete.* They don't harden overnight once you have made them. They are malleable—you can change them and rearrange them as you need to.

Like a good sailor, you allow for the wind, you trim the sails a bit, pull in a little slack, and adjust the course as you go. You watch the weather, look for signs, and take instrument readings along the way. After all, the ocean is large, and it's easy to get lost unless you learn to read a compass.

In decision-making, reading the compass means evaluating your decision after you've given it some time to work. You evaluate a decision much the same way as you would evaluate anything else— say a new pizza-flavored toothpaste.

You buy the toothpaste, take it home, and give it a try. After a few days you sit down and ask yourself a few pointed questions: "Is this stuff good? Is it for me? Should I make a change? Should I continue? Is more time needed to judge? Am I satisfied? Should I try the anchovy-flavored gel next time?"

Depending on how you answer those questions,

Improving Your Foresight / 119

you either continue to support the pizza-flavored toothpaste industry or you make plans to switch to something else.

Evaluating a major decision is not much different. Simply set aside a time to review how things are working out. Examine what you did and the effect it is having. Determine whether the result is what you wanted and see if there are any changes you need to make.

Of course, we often go through this evaluation subconsciously, but we need to link it to the actual decision-making process. A little critic inside all of us forever walks around spouting things like, "I don't like this at all. This will never do! Could be better. Could be better."

If we take this same impulse and analyze it consciously, however, we can turn it to good use. When we bring it out in the open and focus on it in a logical way, we learn from our decisions. And we discover knowledge that would otherwise be lost if we didn't make the conscious effort to retrieve it.

An easy way to evaluate a decision is to take a piece of paper and a pencil and simply write down your thoughts. Ask yourself: *What was good about the decision? What was not so good? Could I have done something better? What would I do differently? What have I learned from the decision?*

You will probably discover some useful information regarding any particular decision you evaluate. And you'll probably learn a few things about the way you make decisions in general.

You might find, for example, that you need to spend more time gathering information and examining choices before deciding. Maybe you are putting too much weight on certain emotional aspects of your decisions. Perhaps you need to take more time in prayer and waiting. Possibly you should do more brainstorming, or be more specific as you think the plan through. You might discover any number of other details about your decision-making method.

The point is that if you don't provide yourself with this little heart-to-heart evaluation of your decision-making system, you doom yourself to wander through life learning little from your decisions and repeating your mistakes time and time again. To break the cycle, you need to do what highly paid corporate executive decision-makers all do—take a step back at a prearranged time and analyze your decision with a cold, objective eye. Take it apart, like an inquisitive inventor, and see which parts worked and which parts didn't. Then take the necessary steps to make the next decision a better one.

By including an evaluation step after your decision-making process, you gradually become better at making decisions. You create a standard against which all future decisions can be measured. You improve your foresight. (Improve it enough, and your friends will think you've learned how to tell the future.) But there's no magic involved, just honest, hard-working reason.

"Wonderful!" you say, "Great! But what do you do when you find yourself stuck in the quicksand of a bad decision?" To answer that question we'll have to ask the experts—the *sports* experts.

12
FOLLOW THROUGH

Baseball stars, golfers, tennis champs, and handball players know that it isn't enough just to hit the ball—you have to follow through. You can't quit when you make contact. You have to continue the motion of the swing through the point of contact to its conclusion.

It is follow-through that gives the swing its power and control. You can't hit home runs without it. You can't make good decisions without it, either. Once you have made your decision, you have to follow through.

Following through on a decision might mean different things in different situations. But in terms of a general definition, you can describe it in one word: *integrity* ("the firm adherence to a code of moral values"). As Christian decision-makers we are to let the moral code of Christ fill our hearts and minds. We adhere to Christ's values.

The definition also includes the suggestion of resolution—of seeing something through to its end, of firmness of purpose. That resolution is also part of good decision-making.

Building on the Rock

Jesus told a story about two men who built houses. (See Matthew 7:24-27.) One man built his house on a rock; the other built on the sand. The rains came, and the streams rose and flooded. The house built on the sand was battered to pieces and washed away. The house built on the rock stood strong and firm.

It makes a tremendous difference what kind of foundation you build your life on. Do you build on sand? Or are you building on the rock?

Sadly, a lot of people appear to be building on cheap beach sand. You can see the ruined remains of their houses washing out to sea after every little storm.

You would think that after a person lost one house to a tidal wave he would learn his lesson and rebuild on the rock. But it hardly ever works that way. As soon as the sun is out again, those slow learners go back to the beach and build another doomed house on the worthless sand.

"That's too bad," you say. "But what does all this have to do with decision-making?"

The rock and the sand stand for the base of integrity the decision-maker builds on. The rock symbolizes the firmness of purpose, the determined resolution, and the quiet inner strength of a soul resting on God. The sand represents the shifting emotions, the uncommitted hesitance, and the weakness of will of a soul anchored only to its own selfish gratification.

The kind of foundation on which we build—whether rock or sand—affects the decisions we make. And as we have seen, decisions form the basic framework of our lives. Christians are to build on the rock. One way to do that is by committing yourself to follow through on your decisions.

The Tie That Binds

Did you ever have a friend promise to meet you at a certain place at a certain time—and then not show up? Or did you agree to work together on a project, but as the deadline for completion drew near discover that you were working all by your lonesome?

These things happen all the time, and they put a strain on even the best friendships. "No big deal," you say. "It happens. Don't try to make a federal case out of it."

But it *is* a big deal—the biggest. Here's why: *The way you handle "little deals" in life will determine how you will handle the "big deals" when you face them.* Jesus said that, "Whoever can be trusted with very little can also be trusted with much, and whoever is dishonest with very little will also be dishonest with much" (Luke 16:10).

124 / Decisions! Decisions! Decisions!

Our integrity hinges on the so-called "little" things of life: a broken promise, a lie told as an excuse, a secret revealed. These and all the other "little" events like them define what kind of people we are. So our integrity depends on our ability to make good decisions.

Every little act of the will, every agreement, every promise, and every action is preceded by a decision. At some point you decide to make the promise, to commit the act, or to enter into the agreement.

The moral condition of the world today makes it difficult for most people to even care about the integrity of their decisions. After all, nearly everyone around you is convinced that agreements, promises, and commitments are useful *only* as long as they give personal pleasure. How can you hang on to your integrity without looking like a fool?

But as Christians, we are to take our decisions seriously—especially when they involve others. Once we make a decision, we should trust in God's guiding presence and follow through on it. Even when it hurts.

That's right. We should be committed to our decisions, and not try to sidestep or back out of them. In making such decisions we are in effect making contracts which we are obligated to carry out, regardless of how we may feel about them later.

Marriage is one good example. A decision to get married is a binding decision. After the ceremony you may do a lot of things, but one thing you may *not* do is back out. No matter how you feel about your decision in the months that follow—after the honeymoon is over and you face the reality of actually having to live with this other person for the rest of your life—you are bound to follow through.

This viewpoint is not a popular one today, where remaining faithful to *anything* is seen as more than just a little fanatical. Student loans are a case in point. The government has found that fewer and fewer people obligate themselves to repay their college loans. As a result, the government is owed many millions of dollars.

It seems that many students who decide to take out a loan for their education simply decide not to repay it. Perhaps they pay it back if they feel they got a decent education. If not, they don't.

Very few seem to consider their loans an issue of morality. Like marriage, repaying loans has lost its moral basis. Two people decide to get married, and later decide to get *un*married. A student promises to pay back money he has borrowed. Then he decides not to. The moral issue has been lost in the shuffle—even for many Christians.

But each of those acts began with a decision, so decision-making itself is elevated to a position of moral significance. Your decision is the tie that binds you to the acts you perform.

Making the Best of a Bad Decision

All this integrity stuff sounds great, and we all know Christians should be moral. But what hap-

126 / Decisions! Decisions! Decisions!

pens when you make a mistake? How do you handle the situation?

Bad decisions do happen, and sometimes they are not the fault of the decision-maker at all. As we saw in the last chapter, we can't always know how things are going to turn out. Bad things can happen even to the most diligent and faithful people. What then?

You make the best of it. Making the best of a bad decision might mean different things in different situations. A lot depends on whether other people are involved, even a little bit, in your decision.

Chapter 11 began with three examples of decisions that backfired. Let's look at them again and see what the individuals might have done to make the best out of the bad results.

Janet's decision to enter nursing school backfired when she found she was not as prepared as the other students and could not keep up. Mike had worked hard to save his money for a much-needed car, only to discover that the car was a lemon. Jean, who wanted to get out on her own, had a bad experience with a roommate who used her and then skipped out. How can these people handle their situations properly?

For Janet, the solution could take several forms. The problem wasn't really her fault. She just hadn't taken the proper courses in high school. So she could talk to the dean, explain her situation, and ask to withdraw mid-term. Then she could transfer to a junior college long enough to pick up the background courses she needed. Or she could get tutoring, finish the year, and then decide where to go from there.

No one else is likely to be directly affected by Janet's decision to stay in nursing school or leave. Her decision does not depend on any spiritual or moral considerations that would prevent her from adjusting her previous decision, changing course, and heading off in a slightly different direction.

Mike has fewer options. About all he can do is try to return the car and get his money back. If the used car dealer refuses, and if there was no wrongdoing involved, then Mike is probably stuck. He must grit his teeth and bear the hurt.

Jean too has fewer options. Since she signed a lease, she cannot move out without losing a large chunk of money. She could talk to the landlord, explain her situation, and hope he would understand. But if he refused to help her, she would have to stick it out until the lease was up. In the meantime, she could try and get another (hopefully better) roommate.

We become people of integrity only when our actions have integrity. And our actions will not have integrity until we view decision-making as a serious moral undertaking.

This May Hurt a Little

Decision-making *is* a serious moral undertaking. Its foundation is God's incredible gift of free will. We have a sacred trust from God to use this gift wisely. Since we are to have the mind of Christ, we should also reflect the integrity of Christ.

128 / Decisions! Decisions! Decisions!

Psalm 15 in the Old Testament begins with a question. "Lord, who may dwell in Your sanctuary? Who may live on Your holy hill?" The psalm then goes on to describe this perfect citizen of God's holy city. Among other attributes it says that this person is one who, "keeps his oath even when it hurts" (v. 4). In other words, this is a person who keeps his promises—regardless of the results. He stays on course, not swerving or trying to weasel out of difficulty.

The Bible is saying that God values moral integrity in His people. Along with truth, justice, and kindness, He desires His followers to develop the inner strengths of purpose and commitment.

Strength of purpose and commitment are what I mean by follow-through. It is the courage to move out in faith and put decisions into action, trusting God to lead and guide. It is *not* fretting our lives away with indecision, doubt, and worry. Nor is it tentatively moving in one direction, only to abandon course as soon as the wind shifts.

Sometimes we find ourselves in difficulty because of the results of a decision. No one, including God, expects us to persist doggedly and let our stubbornness get us into more trouble. That's not what strength of purpose means at all. But sometimes after a decision we find ourselves in circumstances which we would never have chosen—like Janet at a too-tough nursing school, Mike with his worthless car, or Jean with her flaky roommate. In such circumstances we are to take responsibility for our decisions and for our actions—even when the results hurt.

Decisions are the moral stepping-stones which we use to cross life's turbulent waters. And since our decisions affect others, we are to make them wisely and carry them out with integrity. Moving ahead with confidence is a sign of good follow-through.

Cold Feet

Follow-through is important for another reason. Fixing your sights on the road ahead and moving out in faith is a good way to avoid getting cold feet. Psychologically, there is usually an emotional letdown after a major decision.

We can again use the example of a nervous bridegroom who, after deciding to get married, tries on the day of his wedding to find loopholes in the vows. Salesmen are familiar with similar consumer behavior, which they call "buyer's remorse." Immediately after a major purchase a person will often experience feelings of doubt and regret. "I never should have done it. I never should have spent all that money."

The same phenomenon occurs after decision-making. Following any major decision you can expect to experience feelings of doubt, regret, anxiety, and even sorrow. You begin second-guessing yourself: *Did I do the right thing? What if I've made the wrong decision? I'm sure this is the wrong thing to do! I'm doomed!*

As bad as they seem, these feelings are normal. They are a part of the leftover emotional energy that went into making the choice. If you don't listen to these feelings they will soon go away, leaving you with a fairly normal life again.

Using a logical method of decision-making like the one described in this book can help you through the "cold feet" period. When your decisions are based on logic and reason, are thought through prior to being put into effect, and are yielded to any spiritual considerations that apply, you have the necessary ammunition to shoot down all the arguments your fleeting negative emotions can come up with.

When the doubts come, you can simply point to the well-founded research that went into your decision. You can pull out your balance sheet, recall exactly how the decision was made, and take another look at all the reasons why this is your best decision. In the face of logic and reason, "buyer's remorse" doesn't stand a chance.

Some People Have All the "Luck"

Have you ever wondered why things always seem to go right for some people? Why some seem to get all the "lucky" breaks, while nothing seems to go right for other people?

Could it be that the ones with all the "luck" are the ones who have learned to make sound decisions? And that the others who are forever limping from one mess to another are victims of their own poor decision-making habits? I think so.

You make your decisions, but they also make

Follow-through / 131

you. In other words, *the kind of person you become depends on the decisions you make throughout your lifetime.* The more good, rational decisions you make, the more likely you are to have better opportunities in the future. Good things begin to happen when you approach the major decisions in life calmly, with trust in God, and with a sense of purpose.

On the other hand, a person who rushes every decision, acts according to his emotions, and never stops to think or plan cannot help but experience some bad results. If good decision-makers are like moving ships, bad ones are like boats adrift with their sails flapping, or that have run aground and smashed on the rocks.

Life is a lengthy, ongoing journey. You will face decisions every step of the way. The decisions of youth will affect the decisions of adulthood, which in turn will affect the decisions of old age. Decisions never end. You won't outgrow them. So one of the best things you can do for yourself and for your future is to take the time now to learn to make good decisions.

God calls each of us to specific places and purposes in life. For every Christian it is a pilgrimage of faith. But like good, practical pilgrims we are to prepare ourselves for the journey. We hear God more clearly when we are prepared.

I want to leave you with a promise and a challenge: "In his heart a man plans his course, but the Lord determines his steps" (Proverbs 16:9). The promise is that God will always be with you, guiding you and giving direction throughout your decision-making process. Trust Him to direct your steps. The challenge is that you will apply the principles you have learned in this book to "plan your course." Use your mind, reason through the problems, and make the best choices you can.

The decision is yours.